BRADY

EMS Field Training Officer

Robert G. Nixon, BA, EMT-P
Life Care Medical Training

Upper Saddle River, New Jersey 07458

Library of Congress Cataloging-in-Publication Data

Nixon, Robert G.
EMS field training officer / Robert G. Nixon.
p. cm.
ISBN 0-13-049285-X
1. Emergency medical services—Study and teaching. I. Title. RA645.5 .N595 2004
616.02'5'071—dc21

2003012692

Publisher: Julie Levin Alexander
Publisher's Assistant: Regina Bruno
Senior Acquisitions Editor: Katrin Beacom
Assistant Editor: Kierra Kashickey
Senior Marketing Manager: Katrin Beacom
Channel Marketing Manager: Rachele Strober
Director of Production and Manufacturing: Bruce Johnson
Managing Production Editor: Patrick Walsh
Manufacturing Buyer: Pat Brown
Production Liaison: Julie Li
Production Editor: Wendy Druck, *The GTS Companies*/York, PA Campus
Creative Director: Cheryl Asherman
Cover Design Coordinator: Christopher Weigand
Cover Designer: Christopher Weigand
Cover Image: Mark Ide
Compositor: *The GTS Companies*/York, PA Campus
Printer/Binder: Phoenix Color Corporation
Cover Printer: Phoenix Color Corporation

Photo Credits: Credits and acknowledgments borrowed from other sources and reproduced, with permission, appear in this textbook on pp 14, 16, 21, 22, 53, 87, 88, 89, 90, 109, 120, Courtesy of EES Publications. All photos courtesy of Robert G. Nixon.

Pearson Education LTD.
Pearson Education Singapore Pte. Ltd
Pearson Education Canada, Ltd
Pearson Education—Japan
Pearson Education Australia PTY, Limited
Pearson Education North Asia Ltd
Pearson Educaçion de Mexico, S.A. de C.V.
Pearson Education Malaysia, Pte. Ltd

10 9 8 7 6 5 4 3 2 1
ISBN 0-13-049285-X

Contents

Preface

Now there is a book for the rest of us—those in emergency medical service (EMS) education who do not teach at the community college or vocational–technical school. The field training officer is that person who works in the training section of the EMS agency and serves as the field employees' instructor and trainer and may hold the title of chief of training, training coordinator, or field training officer. In some situations, training responsibilities are given to the supervisor rather than having a special position dedicated to training. In such cases, the role of the supervisor has been tremendously expanded.

The classroom may be an actual classroom at the agency's headquarters, or it could be a conference room, the firehouse bay, a dining room table, or, most likely, the back of the ambulance. Although many field training officers may also work in a college setting, many are serving their EMS agencies in the field. It is with those individuals in mind that this textbook is written.

Being a field training officer means that you have accepted the responsibility of teaching new employees about their job and providing continuing education or perhaps refresher training for veteran employees. But being a field training officer is a lot more than merely teaching. It is also being a manager—a supervisor—who looks after and guides the employee as he or she begins or continues a career.

A teacher is someone who molds another person. You will guide the employee along the correct path, providing the tools needed to succeed. You will also evaluate the employee's performance, making suggestions on how to improve knowledge and skills.

The information contained in this book is aimed at giving you the necessary tools to be that teacher and supervisor. Without the basic tools, it would be a guessing game as to what you will need to provide a sound educational foundation for an employee. Consider building a house. If you were told, "Here are the materials. Go build a house," you would probably have trouble if you did not have the tools with which to build the house. The same thing is true about supervising and training an employee. Without the necessary tools, you would not know where to begin or how to accomplish the task.

This book is divided into five sections, with chapters within each section. Most of these sections have self-assessment tools that help you understand yourself, your thoughts, and attitudes. By knowing more about yourself, you can be a better teacher of others.

Section I, "The Art of Being Human" presents information on human behavior. By understanding human behavior and what motivates people, you will have the tools that you can use to effectively teach employees.

Section II, "Communication" gives information on effective communications between you and an employee. The material also discusses blocks to communications. As a side benefit, it will present communication tools that you can use off the job and in your personal life.

Section III, "Management" presents information on managing others. It defines management and discusses various aspects of supervising others.

Section IV, "On Being a Teacher" discusses many of the principles of education. You will be shown the differences between teaching children and adults as well as understand how people learn. This section will also present thoughts on how the field training officer can serve his or her employer as a performance consultant. In addition, information on how to develop goals and objectives to properly and effectively evaluate the new employee's performance will be presented.

The Appendixes, "Lesson Plans, Checklists, Performance Evaluation Review, Worksheet, and Sample Orientation" give samples of lesson plans that can be used as formats for training programs. They also contain sample skills sheets along with an example of a performance evaluation review. Although a performance evaluation review may not be a primary role of the field training officer, he or she may have input into an employee's periodic or annual evaluation.

In these five sections, you will be given information that will enable you to be a skillful teacher.

A Skillful Teacher

When a superior man knows the causes which make instruction successful, and those which make it of no effect, he can become a teacher of others. Thus, in his teaching, he leads and does not drag; he strengthens and does not discourage; he opens the way but does not conduct to the end without the learners' own efforts. Leading, and not dragging, produces harmony. Strengthening and not discouraging makes attainment easy. Opening the way and not conducting to the end makes the learner thoughtful. He who produces such harmony, easy attainment, and thoughtfulness may be pronounced a skillful teacher. (Confucius, Book XVI, Record on the Subject of Education)

Acknowledgments

No book can ever become a reality without the help of a number of people. I would like to thank, first and foremost, John Bird, head of Bay Trans who inspired the idea that became a book when he wanted his field training officers trained for the job. With the initial course and several thereafter, the textbook began to take shape. I would also like to thank Gina Dano with Aetna, Inc., who afforded me the opportunity to become involved with corporate training and expand my professional horizons in performance consulting as well as instructional design.

A debt of gratitude goes to EMS Expo staff, especially Marie Nordberg, who supported the concept of a preconference seminar for field training officers. Additionally, I would like to thank the many EMTs and paramedics who attended the field training officer seminars over the years and allowed me to "field test" and refine the text. This same debt of gratitude goes to the reviewers for Brady who gave insightful comments that served to make the book better.

Finally, there are a lot of people behind the scenes who offered support and assistance along the way. Of special importance is my significant other, Teena Foote, who offered proofreading and suggestions to make the material more understandable.

To all of those who helped make this text become a reality, I say a heartfelt **thank you!**

DEDICATION

The book is dedicated to all of the training officers whose classroom is the "field." Remember, in contrast to what is said, "Those who can, do. Those who can do better, teach."

I

The Art of Being Human

Who Are You and Who Are They?

PERSONALITY TYPES AND HUMAN BEHAVIOR

By understanding the nature of various personality types, you will be better able to work with others, including co-workers, clients, patients, friends, and family. In your role as a field training officer, you will be better able to help an employee learn about the job. You will also be able to boost employee job satisfaction and, when necessary, provide better job counseling.

This section will identify several personality and behavioral traits that are common in people. Although it is important to understand what makes other people behave certain ways, it is also important to understand what makes you "tick." To do this, there is a series of short quizzes in the appendix that can give you insight into your own personality. When scoring these quizzes, you will learn about yourself, which, in turn, will give you information about other people.

This section examines several aspects of human behavior, including:

- Personality types
- Locus of control
- Right-brain versus left-brain thinking
- Maslow's hierarchy of needs
- Strokes
- Hidden motivators

1

Nature of the Person

Personality Types

There are numerous personality types that choose emergency medical services (EMS) as a career. Many of these different personalities fit nicely into the profession although some others may have a tough time adapting to the demands of the job. This chapter will focus on a few of the assessment tools and personality types to enable the field training officer to better understand and work with the employees.

MYERS-BRIGGS PERSONALITY TYPE INDICATOR

The Myers-Briggs Personality Type Indicator is a widely used tool in identifying various personalities. It was developed by Isabel Myers and her mother, Katharine Briggs, and is based upon Carl Jung's psychological types. Unfortunately, it cannot identify personality traits, moods, skills, or abnormal conditions. The indicator has a very high degree of accuracy and is widely used throughout business.

The Myers-Briggs Personality Type Indicator test is available at no cost on the Internet at the following addresses:

Humanmetrics at http://www.humanmetrics.com/cgi-win/JTypes1.htm

Advisor Team at http://www.advisorteam.com/temperament_sorter/register.asp?partid=1

According to the Myers-Briggs Personality Type Indicator, people are placed into eight different categories. These are:

Extroversion	**I**ntroversion
Sensing	**IN**tuition
Thinking	**F**eeling
Judging	**P**erceiving

What These Types Mean

Extroversion

Prefers multiple contacts and is not shy in a group of people

Can function easily in groups and is not timid when meeting new people

Is outgoing and gregarious

EMS personalities may be extroverted, especially if the person enjoys large numbers of people.

Introversion

Prefers one-on-one contacts and tends to be shy

Quiet and reserved in groups

Thinks internally

Prefers to be alone

It may surprise you to learn that many EMS professionals are introverted. They are comfortable when functioning with one partner in a one-on-one situation, as in most instances of patient care.

Sensing

Tends to be detail oriented

Uses all senses to recognize problems

Good at numbers, facts, focused work, and troubleshooting

The sensing EMS professional is acutely aware of his or her surroundings, using the senses to quickly detect problems or hazards.

INtuition

Likes work that involves concepts or theories

Can see the "big picture" and how things fit into the whole

Good at abstract relationships between things

Tends to trust "gut" feelings

An EMT or paramedic who is intuitive may tell you that he or she senses something is not quite right, that there is something more to the call, patient, or situation than meets the eye.

Thinking

Makes objective decisions

Tends to be logical and rational

Best at work that involves logic and problem solving

Can focus on technical problems

The EMS professional who is a thinker functions best in situations that require logic and reason. Problem solving is good when sequential thinking or reasoning is needed.

Feeling

Makes subjective decisions based on "people values"

Tends to focus on the person having the problem, not the problem itself

The feeling EMT or paramedic has great bedside manner and puts the patient at ease.

Judging

Tends to have control over his or her surroundings

Is a decision maker

Is an organizer

Likes closure of a problem

The judging EMT or paramedic may be a good supervisor, because organization and decision-making capabilities are excellent.

KIERSEY TEMPERAMENT SORTER

Another personality assessment tool is the Keirsey Temperament Sorter, which identifies an individual's disposition to particular attitudes and actions. The assessment was developed by David Keirsey in his book, *Please Understand Me II*. The Keirsey Temperament Sorter test is available at no cost on the Internet at the following address:

Advisor Team at http://www.advisorteam.com/temperament_sorter/register.asp?partid=1

According to Keirsey, there are four temperaments: Artisan, Guardian, Idealist, and Rational.

Artisans prefer an external world, usually in some form of art where they can be spontaneous and see quick results. They have keen senses and prefer the hear-and-now of real-life experiences.

Guardians tend to prefer the home and family, only cautiously exploring the world. When they do explore, they plan and prepare carefully. Guardians tend to be the backbone of society and have a stabilizing force.

Idealists tend to care deeply about their fellow man and tend to offer assistance to those in need. They also believe in self-improvement and strive to help others achieve their goals.

Rationals are problem solvers. They look for ways to overcome obstacles and have a tremendous desire to learn how things work. Rationals are inquisitive and are always seeking information.

How do we fit in regarding the thinking or feeling aspect of personality? EMTs and paramedics tend to be thinkers—we focus on the problem and make decisions based most often on logical and rational conclusions. Although we care about the patient, we tend to look beyond the person and get to the nature of the problem.

Are we more judging or perceiving? We may be a little of both—judges and perceivers. We take control over our surroundings, we are reasonably organized in our response to the situation, and we like closure (packaging the patient) during our care of the sick or injured person. However, we are flexible and adaptive to the situation and surroundings. We gather information about the patient, make treatment decisions, and transport the patient to the hospital. After turning the patient over to the emergency department staff and completing our paperwork, we rarely inquire about the status of the patient during subsequent visits to the hospital.

What temperament does the EMS profession have? The more common types that become involved in EMS are the guardians and idealists. Guardians are caregivers, whereas Idealists want to help others. Idealists may also become involved in education and training to offer professional development for themselves and others.

SUMMARY

Although not everyone will fit perfectly into a label or descriptive category, there are specific personality traits that we can identify that will facilitate teaching the individual. For example, an introverted person would not feel comfortable giving a demonstration to a group of colleagues on a particular skill; however, an extroverted person might enthusiastically respond to such a request. The field training officer may not be able to administer the Myers–Briggs Personality Inventory to each EMT and paramedic employed by the agency, but you might be able to recognize and adapt to some of the unique traits displayed by the person you are training.

It is important to always remember that there are many things that go into a person's psychological makeup. One self-assessment does not give anyone a complete picture, but it can give some insight into a person's behavior and a way to help motivate him or her.

2

Locus of Control

Are You Externally Motivated or Internally Motivated?

People are motivated by many different factors—often just meeting basic needs will drive some behaviors. However, people do enjoy getting rewarded for the jobs that they do. The question arises about the type of reward that will keep the person productive and focused on the job. Generally, there are two types of rewards—internal and external—that may give a person an extra boost. The key difference is simple: Is the person driven by internal satisfaction, or does the person believe that he or she has no control over events and, thus, responds to kudos from external sources? The purpose of this chapter is to identify the difference between an internal (intrinsic) reward and one that is external (extrinsic).

LOCUS OF CONTROL

Depending on your view of life, you might believe that your life is pretty much a crapshoot or one in which you call the shots. You might also believe that you are motivated by external factors and things over which you have no control, or that you are motivated by internal gratification.

If you are externally motivated, rewards such as higher pay, commendations, and material things are important to your self-esteem. You also might tend to blame other people or things for your misfortunes, avoiding responsibility for your problems. You might also be "reactive" to events and not see your contribution to a problem.

If you are internally motivated, you tend to take responsibility for yourself; to believe that life is a game of skill rather than chance. Internally motivated people are those who are vigilant about what is going on around them and take control to get a job done. Basically, they believe that their life is in their own hands. This type of person has been described as a self-starter or "proactive," resolving problems at an early stage.

How does the field training officer apply this information to employees? If you know that an employee is externally motivated, then you also know that giving him or her public recognition such as a certificate of achievement or some form of a bonus will stimulate that person to achieve more (think about the name board with stars for achievement). This type of person will need something to hold to be satisfied that a job was done well (or that learning was completed).

In contrast, an internally motivated person gets more satisfaction from knowing that the job was done well than by any external means. Verbally praising the internally motivated person will invite a better response than giving him or her a certificate of achievement.

SUMMARY

It is important to remember that a person is not totally externally or internally motivated. Most of us tend to like some reward for a job well done. Praise is important, but so is occasionally getting a certificate of achievement. Use each judiciously and you will be surprised how a trainee responds. There will be more on motivation later in this section and in the "Management" section.

Right Brain Versus Left Brain

Which Side of Your Brain Calls the Shots?

Your brain consists of two hemispheres—the right side and the left side. Each part of the brain communicates with the other through a network of nerves and connections. However, each person tends to think and perceive with one hemisphere of the brain more than with the other. In other words, that person tends to use the right or left side of the brain more often. The purpose of this chapter is to invite awareness of the differences between right and left brain thinking so that you will have a better understanding of how a person learns. This information will be especially helpful when a problem in learning is found. As a field training officer, you can adjust your teaching techniques to suit the situation and enhance the trainee's ability to grasp information.

Before continuing with any further discussion, find the right brain versus left brain self-assessment below. After completing and scoring the quiz, see for yourself which side of your brain "calls the shots," or is the dominant side for processing information.

RIGHT-BRAIN VERSUS LEFT-BRAIN THINKING

Read each question carefully. Choose answer a or b based on your preferences at least 51 percent of the time. Do not attempt to analyze or argue with any of the questions.

1. Think of your favorite song. Close your eyes and let it run through your head for 10 to 15 seconds. Did you focus more on:
   a. the words?
   b. the melody?
2. You are at a restaurant with a friend and he asks you for directions to get somewhere. Do you:
   a. write out step-by-step instructions?
   b. draw a map?
3. When you buy audio equipment—stereo, radio, CD player, etc., do you:
   a. carefully analyze all the available specifications, data, and statistics, familiarizing yourself with electronic concepts important to the understanding of the spec sheets?
   b. listen to the components in the systems in your price range and choose one for the quality of the sound and appearance of the equipment?

4. When you are hung up getting started on a project or working out a problem, it is because:
   a. you get bogged down in all the details or don't know where to start?
   b. you try to do too many things at the same time and end up with your energies too spread apart, without putting your best abilities to work anywhere?
5. What kind of camera do you prefer?
   a. A manually controlled 35-mm single lens reflex, where you have control over the shutter speed, f-stop, flash, etc.
   b. One that allows you to worry about the picture, not the camera, such as an automatic 33 mm, an "Instamatic," or instant-developing model.
6. Does picture 1 below match better with picture 2 or picture 3?

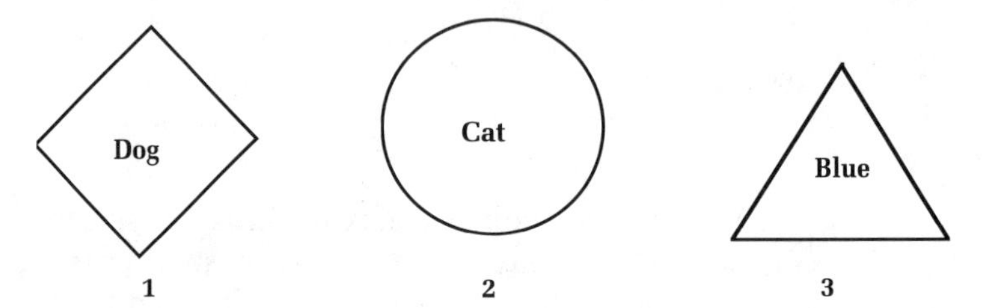

   a. 2.
   b. 3.
7. Are you sold on an idea:
   a. after carefully reading up on it, analyzing the aspects step-by-step?
   b. if you can picture it as a success, if it "grabs" you, or if you get an intuitive, gut feeling that it will go?
8. Do you judge a person by:
   a. what he or she says?
   b. his or her eye contact, body language, and appearance?
9. When it comes to spectator sports, are you better at:
   a. keeping score, remembering player averages, records, etc.?
   b. mapping out play strategies, anticipating where the action will be?
10. Does picture 1 below match better with picture 2 or picture 3?

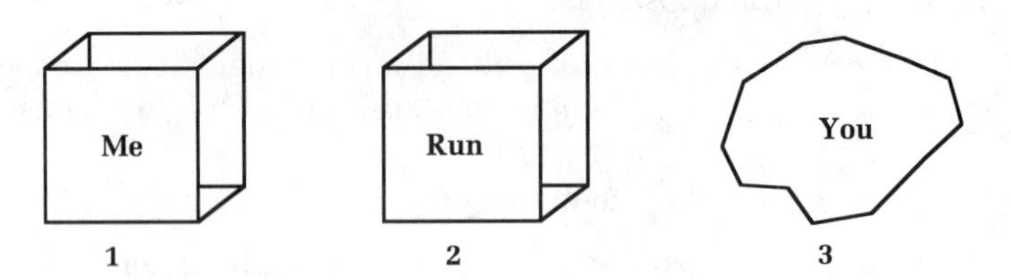

   a. 2
   b. 3
11. Do you work better when:
   a. you can do the specialized work that you are best at, analyzing it and making it all add up, without distractions?
   b. you can see how your work plugs into the big picture or if you are involved in interpreting patterns and viewpoints of the whole picture?

12. How do you keep your desk, the place where you work, your hobby room, or garage?
    a. Neat and orderly. Everything has its place. If it gets cluttered, you can't find anything.
    b. It's a mess, but you can find anything you need. If someone should clean it up, you'd be lost.
13. Recall what you had for dinner yesterday. Close your eyes and remember the meal for 5 seconds. Did you:
    a. recite the list of the foods, using words to describe them?
    b. picture the image of the meal in your mind, including the smells and tastes of the food?
14. When you work on a project, do you prefer to:
    a. have all the facts so you can analyze them carefully and plan the best sequence of steps for implementing it?
    b. get started right away, as soon as you have a feel for it—diving in and figuring you can always plug the gaps later?
15. When you put something together, like a game, toy, or new piece of equipment, do you:
    a. carefully follow the written instructions, step-by-step, to the letter?
    b. try to eyeball it and figure out on your own how to put it together, perhaps glancing at the instructions if you get stuck?
16. Would you rather describe an object or a place by:
    a. writing a complete description?
    b. drawing a simple sketch?
17. When you buy something to read while on vacation, do you:
    a. take it with you and read while others are swimming or sunning themselves?
    b. end up hardly reading at all because you just let go and have fun?
18. Does picture 1 match better with picture 2 or picture 3?

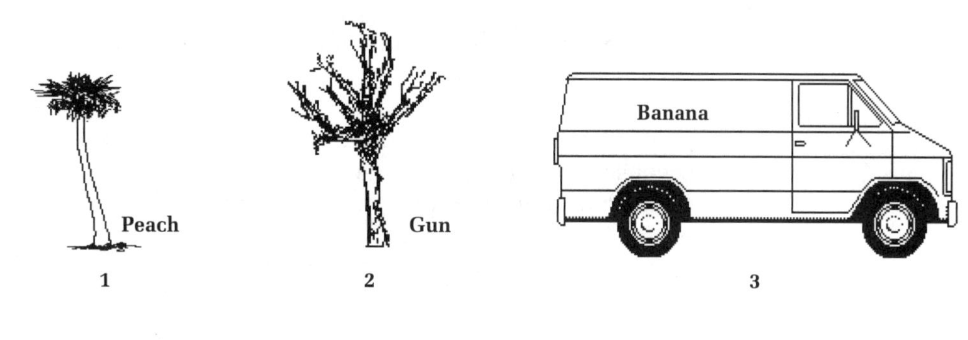

    a. 3.
    b. 2.

Scoring Right-Brain Versus Left-Brain Thinking

Count the number of times you answered a and the number of times you answered b. Place your score in the spaces below.

a ____________ b____________

Left-brain thinking is indicated by a, whereas b indicates right-brain thinking. If you scored higher in one category, you tend to use that particular side of your brain when seeing things or thinking. If you scored evenly (within one or

2 points on either side), you tend to be able to switch back and forth between the left and right sides of your brain. Refer to the discussion below for a description of the characteristics of each half of your brain.

Each side of the brain has a specific nature. Below are the attributes for each hemisphere:

Left Brain	Right Brain
Verbal: Uses words to describe, define	Nonverbal: Minimal connection with words
Analytic: Figuring it out step-by-step	Synthetic: Putting things together to form whole
Symbolic: Using symbols to represent something	Concrete: Relating to things as they are at present
Abstract: Using a small bit of information to represent all	Analogic: Seeing likenesses between things
Temporal: Keeping track of time, sequencing	Nontemporal: Without a sense of time
Rational: Conclusions based on reason, fact	Nonrational: Not requiring a basis of reason, fact
Digital: Using numbers as in counting	Spatial: Seeing things in relation to other things
Logical: Conclusions based on logic	Intuitive: Leaps of insight based on feelings
Linear: Thinking in terms of linked ideas	Holistic: Seeing whole things at once

As previously mentioned, knowing this information can make teaching a person easier. For example, a left-brain-dominant person has trouble reading a map and, when asked to find a location on a map, may become totally confused. Teaching the left-brain-dominant person map-reading skills becomes a task in step-by-step procedures.

In contrast, teaching a right-brain-dominant person the step-by-step processes of loading a patient into the ambulance might become exasperating, because the right-brain person has trouble with logical sequences. Letting the right-brain-dominant person see the end result, and then backtracking, using a proper sequence, might help him or her to understand the process. These concepts will be discussed in more detail in section IV, "On Being a Teacher."

SUMMARY

Although no one is totally right-brain or left-brain dominant, it is important to note the differences. When instructing a person on content or a skill and they look confused, you may want to realign your teaching style to the hemisphere of the brain they use more often to process information.

The Needs That Drive

Maslow's Hierarchy of Needs, Strokes, and Drivers

A lot of our behavior is based on fulfilling the needs that we have and how secure we feel in having those needs met. If we have a strong need that is not being fulfilled, we are motivated, if not driven, to satisfy that need. In 1954, Abraham Maslow identified a set of needs that each person has that will motivate the person to achieve certain things, that is, meet those needs. These needs, according to Maslow, are critical in our survival and ongoing existence.

Before discussing Maslow's hierarchy of needs, it is important to define the term *need* as opposed to *want*. A need is something you must have to survive. For example, food is a need, as is water. Without food or water our survival is questionable. A want is something desirable, but it is something that you can survive without. An example of a want is a new car. You might want a new vehicle, but you can live without one.

Maslow identified five basic needs that motivate people. They include basic physiologic needs, safety and security, belonging and social needs, esteem and status, and self-growth and actualization (see the illustration that follows). Some authors have illustrated the needs in the shape of a pyramid, with the stronger, foundation needs at the bottom. Another way of viewing the hierarchy is in the shape of a ladder—climbing from one need to the next as each need is met. The first four needs are considered by Maslow as deficit needs. A person will be motivated to fulfill the need as long as that person feels he or she does not have enough of something. For example, if a person does not have enough food, he or she may forego meeting safety needs until the basic physiologic needs have been met. Thus, it is important to note that this is a dynamic process and a person can go back to any section of the pyramid at any time. An equally important reminder is that only when a need has been met will that person strive to the next, higher level of the pyramid.

To understand where an employee may be positioned on the pyramid, take a look at each need. The first step on this pyramid is **basic physiologic needs.** More simply stated, these needs include, but are not limited to, food, water, oxygen, clothing, and shelter. A person must meet these needs in order to survive. As a child, your parents met these needs. However, as an adult, you are responsible for meeting these needs. Getting a job and receiving a paycheck is a way of providing food, clothing, and shelter for the self and family. The new employee might be motivated to do a good job solely on this basis alone, for if he were to lose his job and no longer afford to pay rent or buy food and clothing, he would be struggling for survival.

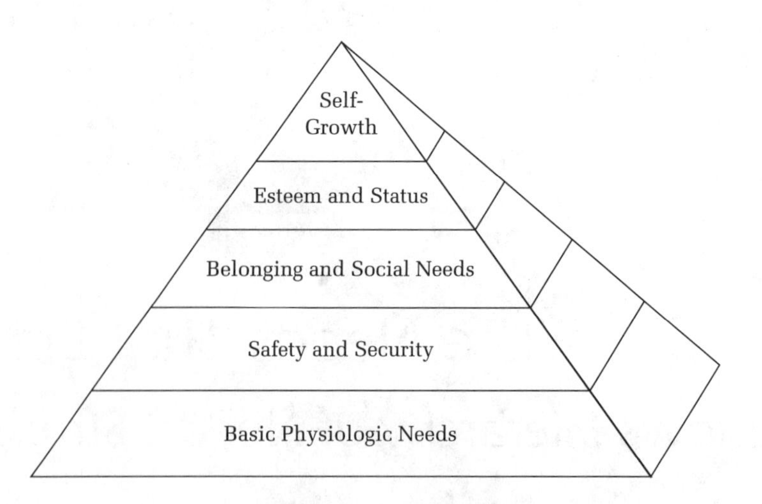

After meeting the basic physiologic needs, the employee can move to the next level in the pyramid; **safety and security.** A person needs to feel safe and secure in his or her employment. Most employers have a probationary period, and new employees will do little to jeopardize their employment during this time. Even if the job is not everything they had expected, most new employees will do little to "rock the boat." Once the probationary period has been completed, the employee can feel a bit safer and attempt to move on to the next level. But can an employee revisit this level even after being on the job for a few years?

As previously mentioned, these first four basic needs are deficit needs. Assume that a four-year veteran of the agency has recently received a promotion and along with that promotion a new probationary period is introduced. He or she is no longer "safe and secure" in that position until the probationary period has been completed. During this time, the newly appointed supervisor will act like any new employee and strive to meet the safety and security need.

Belonging and social needs is the next level. This need can actually be met while the employee is on probation. Every person has the need to feel like they belong or fit in with other employees. They tend to adopt the attitudes of fellow employees and espouse the group's feelings and attitudes, even though they might not totally agree with them. There can be some negative ramifications to this need to belong.

Suppose an employee comes to work with high ideals and the self-imposed demand for excellence on the job. Initially, the employee might perform at his or her highest level. But, depending on the group of peers he or she wants to join, that level could drop. Assume the new employee connects with other employees whose performance levels are considerably lower. In trying to fit in with that group, the new employee must accommodate peer pressure or leave the group. Thus, in trying to fit in, the new employee takes on the attitudes and job performance that he or she thinks the group will accept. This new attitude can pose a problem for the field training officer or supervisor when counseling a new employee on his or her job performance.

After becoming socially accepted by one's peers, a person heads for the fourth level of the pyramid—**esteem and status.** According to Maslow, there are two levels of the esteem and status need—lower and higher. The lower need consists of the need for the respect of others, the need for fame, glory, recognition, and similar accolades. The higher level includes the need for feelings of confidence, competence, and mastery of the skills of the job. Achieving this higher level includes achieving self-respect, which is the reason it is on the higher level of esteem and status—once you achieve self-respect, it is difficult to lose it.

Esteem and status can be met in a variety of ways. Rewards for a job well done, getting a pay increase, receiving a letter or certificate of commendation, or being promoted to a supervisory position are all ways of achieving esteem and status. As a field training officer, you can help motivate employees by recognizing good performance and commending an employee for doing a good job. It is as important to reward good behavior as it is to discourage inappropriate activities.

As was mentioned above, these first four needs are deficit needs—when we do not have enough of something we will strive to get it. We can also view these needs as regulating our behavior like a thermostat. For example, when we get cold, the thermostat kicks in and the furnace heats up. Similarly, when a need is not being met, the drive kicks in as we diligently seek to fulfill that need. In contrast, when things are too hot, the thermostat shuts down and turns off the furnace. Likewise, if every need is being met and a person is satisfied, there is no drive to meet a need (that really does not exist at that time).

If an employee has met esteem and status needs, expecting the employee to go after more kudos and get further recognition while in training would be futile. Motivating that employee to learn might be difficult unless the field training officer is able to tie learning into maintaining the esteem and status currently enjoyed by the employee or perhaps motivating the employee to reach the self-growth and actualization need.

By meeting the need for esteem and status, a person can move to the highest level on the hierarchy of needs—**self-growth and actualization.** This level is the hardest to achieve and consists of recognizing self-worth and overall potential. To meet this need for self-growth and actualization, a person might find him- or herself changing jobs or careers, writing journal articles or books, or obtaining a college degree. To help an employee meet this need, the individual should be encouraged to explore his or her potential to determine personal goals in life. An employer can help meet this need by offering assistance, such as tuition or paid time off.

Maslow identified the special, driving forces behind those who are seeking self-actualization. He labeled these needs as "Being," or B-needs. To be fulfilled, those seeking self-actualization need the following:

Wholeness—Unity, integration, interconnectedness, organization, structure
Perfection—Necessity, just-rightness, inevitability, suitability
Completion—Ending, finality, justice, sense that "it's finished," destiny
Justice—Fairness, orderliness, lawfulness
Aliveness—Process, spontaneity, full functioning
Richness—Differentiation, complexity, intricacy

Simplicity—Honesty, essentiality, abstract
Beauty—Rightness, form, simplicity, richness, perfection
Goodness—Desirability, justice, benevolence, honesty
Uniqueness—Idiosyncrasy, individuality, novelty
Effortlessness—Ease, lack of strain, grace
Playfulness—Fun, enjoyment, amusement, humor, exuberance
Truth—Honesty, reality, simplicity, richness, pure, clean, unadulterated
Self-sufficiency—Autonomy, independence, self-determination

If you have an employee at the self-growth level, think about how you can help that person fulfill these B-needs.

HOW WE CAN HELP

We are all in a state of flux, trying to meet survival needs and searching for safety, security, esteem, and status. The needs identified by Abraham Maslow are like taking steps on the pyramid of life. Meeting each of the needs of life poses many challenges. As a field training officer, you can assist employees in reaching their life's goals through encouragement and commendation. It is important to realize that reaching the next, higher level brings significant changes in a person's life.

GETTING YOUR STROKES—ANOTHER DRIVING FORCE

Previously, we discussed Maslow's hierarchy of needs, looking at factors that help motivate a person to achieve. In addition to having a hierarchy of needs that a person strives to meet, everyone also has a need to be recognized as a person. This recognition comes in the form of "strokes"—a verbal reaffirmation.

The need for strokes develops in infancy. As a baby, your parents, grandparents, other adults, and other children physically touched you. At times you might have cried because you needed to be touched or stroked. This need for a physical touch is a way we reaffirm our existence. But as we age, we modify the need for physical touching into a need for verbal touches.

As we get older, our parents warn us about touching and being touched by other people. But the need for strokes is constant. So we develop a system of nonphysical touching, or verbal stroking. For example, a simple "Hi" is a verbal stroke and is accepted by each person as an affirmation for being.

There are a couple of interesting observations about our stroking system. First, we keep score. We offer one stroke in anticipation of getting one stroke in return. Consider the following verbal exchange by two people walking down a hallway:

You: "Hi. How ya doin'?" (Offering one stroke)
Them: "How ya doin'?" (Giving one stroke back)

You: "Hi. How ya doin'?" (Offering one stroke)
Them: "Great. And you?" (Accepting the stroke and giving one back)
You: "Just fine." (Accepting return stroke)

Consider what happens when the stroke is not returned:

You: "Hi. How ya doin'?" (Offering one stroke)
Them: (Ignoring you—rejects the stroke and doesn't offer one in return)
You: (Thinking, What's wrong with that jerk?)

Or, what happens when you get more strokes back than you offered?

You: "Hi. How ya doin'?" (Offering one stroke)
Them: "Not so good. My cat died and my wife has been sick. And, to top it off, my mortgage is late and my roof is leaking." (Offering four in return)
You: (Thinking, Oh, gad, what did I do to deserve this?)

A second interesting aspect of strokes is the type of strokes that are offered. There are four types of strokes:

- Positive unconditional strokes
- Positive conditional strokes
- Negative unconditional strokes
- Negative conditional strokes

A third aspect of strokes is that the person who gives you the stroke is also important. If the giver is significant in your life, the stroke will have more weight. For example, a mere acquaintance telling you that you are special may not have as much weight as your significant other saying the same thing.

The **positive unconditional stroke** is a verbal touch for existing. The receiver of the stroke did not have to do anything to earn the stroke. Examples of a positive unconditional stroke are "I like you" or "I love you" or "You are a great person." You will notice that there are no conditions attached to those statements.

In the spaces below, list the positive unconditional strokes you have received and from whom they came.

Stroke	**From**
______________________	______________________
______________________	______________________
______________________	______________________
______________________	______________________

In looking over your answers, you can see how important these strokes could be in reaffirming your existence.

A **positive conditional stroke** has conditions attached. In other words, the receiver of the stroke had to do something to get the stroke. Examples of a positive conditional stroke are, "You did a great job splinting that leg" or "Your hair looks nice" or "Dinner was terrific." Notice that there are conditions (splinting, doing the hair, cooking dinner) attached to each stroke.

In the spaces below, list the positive conditional strokes you have received and from whom they came. Consider the impact these strokes had on your mental well-being.

Stroke	**From**
____________________	____________________
____________________	____________________
____________________	____________________
____________________	____________________

Just as there are strokes that say good things, there are strokes that convey negative thoughts. The **negative unconditional stroke** relays negative information to a person. Examples of a negative unconditional stroke are "What a jerk" or "You must be a moron!" Like the positive unconditional stroke, there are no strings attached, no conditions or actions the receiver does to get the stroke. Be aware that negative unconditional strokes can invite resentment in the new employee and pose a barrier to learning.

In the spaces below, list the negative unconditional strokes you have received and from whom they came. Think about how you felt when you received them.

Stroke	**From**
____________________	____________________
____________________	____________________
____________________	____________________
____________________	____________________

A **negative conditional stroke** is a negative stroke given to a person for doing something. Examples of negative conditional strokes are "You really botched that report" or "You shouldn't have dropped that patient" or "You're a lousy driver." Like the positive conditional stroke, there are conditions (writing the report, dropping the patient, driving) attached to the stroke.

In the spaces below, list the negative conditional strokes you have received and from whom they came. Think about how you felt when you received them.

Stroke	**From**
____________________	____________________
____________________	____________________
____________________	____________________
____________________	____________________

Why is it important to know about strokes? People are motivated to receive strokes; they need them to reaffirm their existence. It does not matter what type of stroke the person receives, it is important that he or she receives one. The implications here are significant. If a person receives more positive strokes than negative ones, that person will be motivated to do good things or act according to company policies and procedures. In contrast, if the person receives only negative strokes, he or she will be motivated to make mistakes or act contrary to policies and procedures. In either case, the employee is getting what is wanted—attention. If an employee is misbehaving to get attention and receive strokes, reprimanding the employee will not necessarily end the problem.

Most often, the field training officer will be in a position to offer positive conditional strokes because they are the ones that have "strings" attached. But giving a compliment to someone can be difficult.

In the spaces below, list the positive conditional strokes you can offer an employee and some examples of events, jobs, and achievements for which they may be given.

Stroke	For
______________	______________
______________	______________
______________	______________
______________	______________

How We Can Help

We all need to feel valued, to feel reaffirmed for our very existence. To meet this need, we develop a system of strokes or verbal touches that we actively seek. Without these touches we may fail to thrive. So we behave in such a way to get the strokes that we need. As a field training officer, you can offer positive conditional strokes to help mold the desired behavior and enable the new employee to meet his or her goals and the veteran employee to excel on the job.

THOSE LURKING "HIDDEN DRIVERS"

Behavior is not only motivated by a hierarchy of needs or stroke system; each of us may also have hidden motivators that invite us to act a certain way. These hidden motivators are known as "drivers" and include the Be Perfect Driver, Please Me Driver, Hurry-Up Driver, Try Hard Driver, and the Be Strong Driver.

Before continuing any further, look at the **hidden driver** quiz below. After taking this quiz and scoring yourself, continue reading to gain an understanding into the hidden drivers.

Are There Hidden Drivers?

Read each statement carefully. For each statement below, indicate whether you [4] Strongly Agree, [3] Agree, [2] Disagree, or [1] Strongly Disagree.

	SA	A	D	SD
1. I need to do the best job possible otherwise I am not happy with myself.	[4]	[3]	[2]	[1]
2. No one else can do a job as good as I can.	[4]	[3]	[2]	[1]
3. I have often found that, to get a job done and done well, I better do it myself.	[4]	[3]	[2]	[1]
4. I don't like to ask for help in getting a job done.	[4]	[3]	[2]	[1]
5. If I don't do a good job, people won't like me.	[4]	[3]	[2]	[1]
6. If I am assigned a job and don't do it to the best of my abilities, I will be embarrassed in front of my friends and employees.	[4]	[3]	[2]	[1]
7. I feel the need to help someone else, especially when the job they have is important or difficult.	[4]	[3]	[2]	[1]
8. I enjoy helping other people, especially in times of crisis, such as when they are ill or injured.	[4]	[3]	[2]	[1]

9. When I help someone, I feel a bit better than them. [4] [3] [2] [1]
10. Deadlines are important to me. I need target dates. [4] [3] [2] [1]
11. I will work on a project and get it done on time, even if it means I have to work overtime. [4] [3] [2] [1]
12. Working overtime doesn't bother me, especially if I am paid for it. [4] [3] [2] [1]
13. Whenever I make a mistake, no matter how slight, I get embarrassed or upset. [4] [3] [2] [1]
14. I get defensive when someone criticizes me. [4] [3] [2] [1]
15. If I slip, stumble, or fall while walking, I look around to see if anyone saw me. [4] [3] [2] [1]
16. If I spill something on my clothes, I feel uncomfortable until I am able to change clothes. [4] [3] [2] [1]
17. When someone else slips, stumbles, or falls down, I get the urge to laugh out loud. [4] [3] [2] [1]
18. I don't feel good unless almost everyone likes me. [4] [3] [2] [1]
19. I try hard to make everyone like me. [4] [3] [2] [1]
20. I get upset if someone doesn't like me. [4] [3] [2] [1]
21. I will sometimes compromise my principles just so someone won't be upset or angry with me. [4] [3] [2] [1]
22. If someone doesn't like me, I go out of my way to avoid them. [4] [3] [2] [1]
23. When I am depressed, I will often "act" happy. [4] [3] [2] [1]
24. When I am sad and feel like crying, I will avoid other people. [4] [3] [2] [1]
25. When I am angry, I don't let it show because other people might be upset with me. [4] [3] [2] [1]
26. It's not a good idea to let people know how I feel because they might take advantage of me. [4] [3] [2] [1]
27. I don't share my problems with anyone because they probably don't really care. [4] [3] [2] [1]
28. I take myself seriously. [4] [3] [2] [1]

Scoring the Hidden Motivators

Look at statements 1 through 6. Add the number of points for all of these statements. If your score is between 18 and 24, you have indicated a strong drive to be perfect (**Be Perfect Driver**). You might not tolerate mistakes well and you might have the need to be perfect. You also tend to succumb to the criticism that, while you did a good job, you could have done it better.

Look at statements 7, 8, and 9. Add the number of points for all of these statements. If your score is between 9 and 12, you might have the **Please Me Driver.** You might have the need to please other people to feel good about yourself and validate your self-worth. Look at statements 10, 11, and 12. Add the number of points for all of these statements. If your score is between 9 and 12, you might have the **Hurry-Up Driver.** You might procrastinate in getting things done so that you put yourself under pressure to perform. You might also set yourself up to fail under this pressure.

Look at statements 13 through 22. Add the number of points for all of these statements. If your score is between 30 and 40, you might have the **Try Hard Driver.** The Try Hard Driver means that you want everyone to like you and will try hard to achieve those results, even if it means compromising your values.

Look at statements 23 through 27. Add the number of points for all of these statements. If your score is between 15 and 20, you might have the **Be Strong Driver.** This indicates the need to hide your emotions from people, including the people that you trust the most.

Look at statement 28. If your score is between 3 and 4 points, you've got to be kidding! Keep in mind, the statement did not ask about taking your job responsibilities or personal responsibilities seriously, it only asked if you take *yourself* seriously.

The **Be Perfect Driver** is a hidden motivator to constantly excel in everything you attempt. If you make a mistake, if your clothes are messy, if you get less than an A on your report card, if you get less than outstanding on a performance evaluation review, if you slip, stumble, or fall, then you feel less than adequate. Making a mistake or being less than perfect invites you to mentally "beat yourself up."

However, it is important to realize that there is a difference between *wanting* to excel and *needing* to be perfect. Although there is nothing wrong with wanting to be perfect, being driven to high standards of excellence can, ultimately, be emotionally harmful. You will never see yourself as "good enough." The best way to eliminate this driver is to realize that you are only human and that you will make mistakes and that you are no less a person even if you err.

The **Please Me Driver** is the underlying need to help someone else. Although helping someone in a crisis can be gratifying and, at times, enjoyable, some people enter a helping profession to feel good about themselves. By giving their time and energies to another person, they justify their existence and self-worth. There is a downside to this helping persona. If you do not stop and take some time for yourself and keep giving and giving to other people, your "giver" might finally give out! In essence, you can become burned out on helping others.

The **Hurry-Up Driver** indicates that the you only feel good personally when placed under pressure. You either set unrealistic deadlines that, subconsciously, you know cannot be met, or you procrastinate until the last possible minute. In many cases, individuals set themselves up for failure. Like the other drivers, there are times when we do run late or unrealistic deadlines are set. But if these problems are continual, there can be a hidden motivator at work.

The **Try Hard Driver** is a hidden motivator that drives you to please everyone else or make everyone like you. You go out of your way to avoid confrontation. If someone is displeased with you or does not like you, you will either avoid that person or try to make things right by going along with just about anything they say or want you to do, even if it means compromising your principles.

As with the other drivers, there is a difference between needing and wanting someone to like you. Being driven by the need to make everyone like you is unhealthy because you will discount yourself for the sake of the other person. To combat the try hard driver, you need to recognize that not everyone will like you. Just because someone does not like you does not mean that you are a less worthy person. One way to look at it is, "If they don't like me, I'm sorry, but it's their loss."

The **Be Strong Driver** is the need to constantly hide emotions from other people. Stifling our emotions can be harmful in that repressing your feelings can lead to emotional distress and, perhaps, abnormal behavior. Although you do not want to "wear your heart on your sleeve," there are times when letting another person know how you feel is essential to your mental health.

SUMMARY

Many of us have motivators that we may not recognize. Sometimes they may be overt, and by not meeting the demands of the driver, we may feel anxious or driven to succeed with stronger resolve. This chapter has discussed Maslow's hierarchy of needs, how we get our strokes, and some of our hidden motivators. By understanding a person's needs and that the trainee's motivation may be influenced by any number of things, the field training officer can modify teaching styles or techniques to best suit the employee's current situation. It is not easy to be perceptive or able to modify techniques "on the fly," but the learning experience can be beneficial to both the field training officer and the employee.

THE ART OF BEING HUMAN—SECTION SUMMARY

In this section, we have addressed some of the traits of being human. You have learned about personality types, whether a person is internally or externally motivated, if the right or left side of the brain dominates one's thinking, and if a person has any hidden drivers or motivators. Being familiar with these concepts can enhance your effectiveness as a teacher and supervisor.

II

Communication

Being a field training officer, supervisor, manager, or simply just being a person means that you will share your thoughts, feelings, ideas, wants, and needs with other people. The act of sharing is the act of communicating. The EMS instructor in a community college or vocational–technical school setting will be presenting lessons typically in a lecture, lecture demonstration, or discussion format to a group of fifteen to twenty students. In contrast, although the field training officer may occasionally present in-service classes to large groups of employees, often the field training officer will be in a one-on-one training environment with the employee. This close proximity leads to more personalized communication that may not be seen in the larger classroom setting.

This section, "Communication," will address several things that are involved with sharing ideas, thoughts, and feelings between people. It will also identify some stumbling blocks that we can overcome to enhance interpersonal communication.

5

The Ego States

There have been many theories about how people communicate. One of the most accessible theories was developed in the 1950s by Eric Berne and called transactional analysis (known as TA). According to Berne, when two people meet face-to-face, verbal communication follows. One person says something and the other person responds. Each communication is a transaction, and each person is either the sender or agent of the communication, or its receiver or respondent. The method of examining the transaction is known as transactional analysis.

This chapter will review some of the concepts of TA and how they can apply to the field training officer.

THE THEORY

According to the theories of transactional analysis, the brain acts as a tape recorder and makes a permanent record of life experiences. Although we may "forget" an event, the brain has it stored in permanent memory. Communication is based in these experiences and originate in one of three "ego" states. The ego states are identified as parent, adult, and child. These ego states effect communication based on your life experiences.

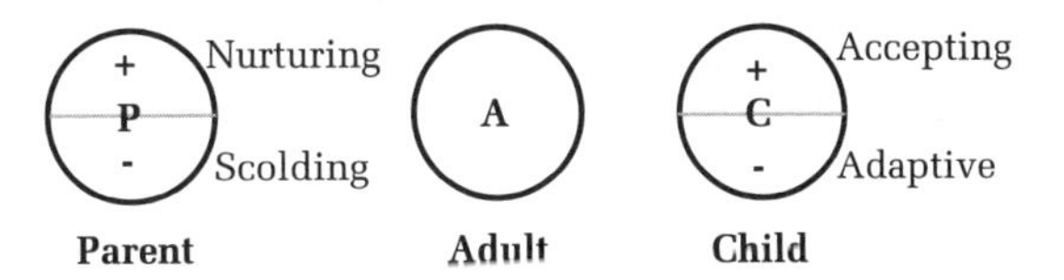

The **parent** ego state provides communication as if it were from your parents or guardians. It is the ingrained voice of authority. When we were young, our parents and significant other adults conditioned us about life. Often, they used phrases such as "Don't lie" or "Under no circumstances." We recorded these messages (and, occasionally, they come out almost verbatim when we are talking to our children). The communication has either a positive (nurturing) or negative (scolding) quality. For example, when telling a child about the hazards of crossing the street, a parent can say, "You need to look both ways to make sure there are no cars coming," which is nurturing. Or, the parent could say, "I told you to look both ways before crossing the street!" which is scolding. Simplistically stated, the parent is the "taught" part of life.

The **adult** ego state means that your communication is coming from the here and now, rational, autonomous state of mind. You process information logically and objectively, stating your thoughts or feelings in a nonprejudicial manner. It is also the way we keep the parent and child ego states under control. Simplistically stated, the adult is the "thought" part of life.

The **child** ego state means that your communication is based on reactions and emotions associated with events that occurred as you developed as a child. Communication under this ego state will be based on the hearing, seeing, feeling, and emotional data stored within the brain. When communication is based on anger or despair, the child ego state is at work. There are two components of the child ego state, accepting (responsive to communication) and adaptive (resistant to communication), which will react depending on how you perceive the initial message. Simplistically stated, the child is the "felt" part of life.

Whenever we communicate with someone, we are using one of these ego states. Similarly, when the other person responds, he or she is also using one of the ego states. In the previous example about crossing the street, consider how communication can develop between the parent and child ego states.

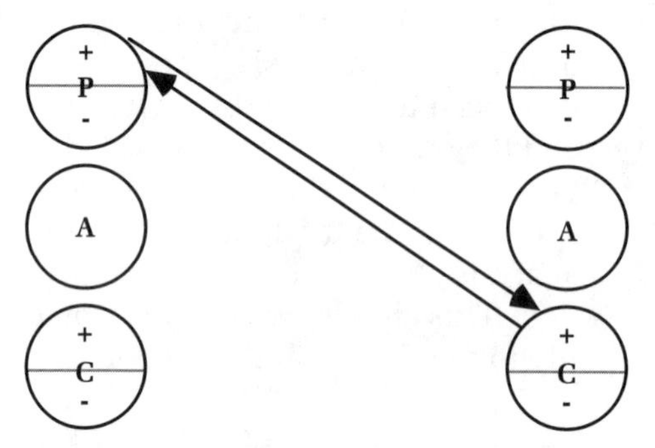

Nurturing parent: "You need to look both ways . . ."
Accepting child: "Yes, Mommy, I'll be careful."

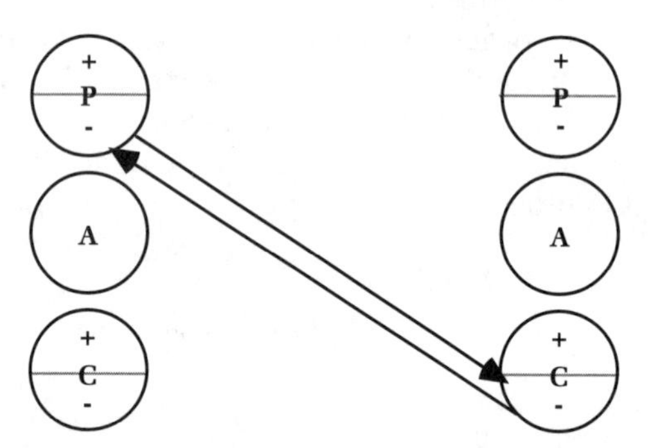

Scolding parent: "I told you to look both ways . . ."
Adaptive child: "You can't tell me what to do!"

The above examples are called complimentary communications in that they are parallel to each other and the lines do not cross. Parent invites child and child responds back to parent.

Here are some sample communications. Identify the ego states for each statement:

What time is it?	Parent	Adult	Child
Let me check your ECG.	Parent	Adult	Child
You are always late for work.	Parent	Adult	Child

Check your answers on the next page.

What time is it?	Parent	**Adult**	Child
Let me check your ECG.	Parent	**Adult**	Child
You are always late for work.	**Parent**	Adult	Child

Now, look at the possible responses and identify the originating ego state.

Stimulus	***Response***		
What time is it?	I am not your keeper. Next time, bring your watch.		
The response is from	Parent	Adult	Child
Let me check your ECG.	Let me unbutton my shirt.		
The response is from	Parent	Adult	Child
You are always late to work.	Give me three examples.		
The response is from	Parent	Adult	Child

Check your answer below.

Stimulus	***Response***		
What time is it?	I am not your keeper. Next time, bring your watch.		
The response is from	**Parent**	Adult	Child
Let me check your ECG.	Let me unbutton my shirt.		
The response is from	Parent	**Adult**	Child
You are always late to work.	Give me three examples of when I was late.		
The response is from	Parent	**Adult**	Child

Problems arise when communication is crossed (see the figure that follows). When this happens, all effective communication is blocked. Occasionally, a condition known as **uproar** develops, which means that although people are talking or sometimes yelling, no one is listening.

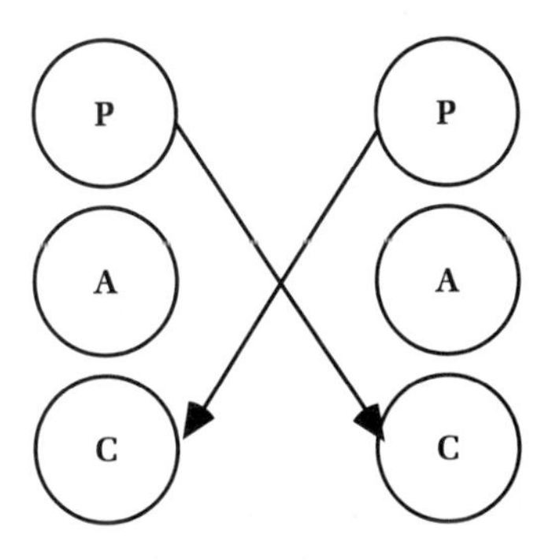

If uproar develops, you need to step back and change ego states. By changing ego states you can, hopefully, redirect the communication and end the uproar. If you cannot redirect the communication, the best recourse is to end the conversation and resume a calmer discussion at a later time.

In order to appropriately change ego states, you need to be aware of the communication. An example of redirecting the conversation is as follows:

You are preparing to transport a patient with chest pain to the emergency department.

You: "Well, Mr. Jones. We are ready to take you to the hospital." (Adult)
Patient: "I'm not going. I don't like hospitals." (Child—You can't make me go.)
You: "You need to get that chest pain checked." (Adult)
Patient: "I'm tired of doctors. All they want is money." (Child—I don't wanna go.)
You: "You need to see the doctor." (Parent)
Patient: "But I don't like doctors." (Child)
You: "Let's go to the hospital or you may get sicker." (Parent)
Patient: "Well, OK. If you say so." (Child)

By changing your ego state, you have actually enhanced communication and achieved the goal of transporting the patient. In this case, the patient needed a parent figure to take charge of the situation.

But how do you know which ego state is being used? There are some physical as well as verbal clues for each ego state:

Parent

Physical clues: Angry or impatient stance or facial expression. Finger pointing. Patronizing gestures.

Verbal clues: Always. Never. "Over my dead body." "If I told you once . . ." "For once and for all . . ." Judgmental or critical language.

Adult

Physical clues: Attentive. Interested. Head tilted. Arms and legs open. Leaning forward. Eye contact.

Verbal clues: Asking what, why, who, where, when, and how. Using phrases such as "I think," "I believe," "I see."

Child

Physical clues: Sad expression. Despair. Temper tantrum. Whining vocal tone. Rolling eyes. Shrugging shoulders. Laughter. Speaking behind hands or fingers. Squirming. Giggling.

Verbal clues: Baby talk. "I wish. . . ." "I don't wanna. . . ." "I don't care." "Worst day of my life." Use of superlatives such as *big, biggest.* Use of words merely to impress.

SUMMARY

In communication, and especially in transactional analysis, listening, seeing, and feeling what is said is key. If communication is not going smoothly, step back, analyze the ego states that originated the communication, and make changes as needed. The field training officer may hear various responses, depending on the training situation. For example, if performing corrective training, expect to hear the parent and child ego states more often than the adult. If the communication is causing some discomfort, anxiety, or frustration, it may be time to think about what is being said and how to modify the conversation.

Gender Differences

Men and women approach communication differently. There are several well-documented differences between the genders in how each communicates, which can pose problems between a field training officer and an employee of the opposite gender. This chapter will address some of the gender differences and how to reduce communication conflicts.

WE ARE DIFFERENT

According to John Gray's very popular book *Men Are from Mars, Women Are from Venus,* one major difference between men and women is that men tend to be *solution oriented*, whereas women tend to be more *process oriented.* A man's sense of self is often defined through his ability to obtain results. When a man senses a problem, his result-oriented mode causes him to propose solutions. For example, if a man hears of a problem such as a bad day at work, he might automatically say, "What you need to do is . . ." or "You can always quit."

A woman's sense of self is often defined through her feelings and the quality of her relationships. When a woman discusses her problems (work, relationships, etc.), she may not want a solution to them. Rather, she may simply want to share her feelings (vent) about her experiences. One way a man and woman can avoid such conflict is to say, at the outset, the intent of the conversation. For example, the woman can say, "I just want you to listen," and the man can ask, "Do you want answers to your problems or just need to vent?"

In addition, according to Gray, men want to feel that they do a good job. The field training officer will inevitably encounter a new or veteran employee of the opposite gender whom she has to retrain or refresh in certain skills. Occasionally, this can create communication conflicts. Since doing a good job is important to the male trainee, changing the man's behavior may require special communication, especially if the field training officer is a woman.

With some male trainees, inviting his active participation in the learning process rather than giving a direct order that he might resist could facilitate cooperation and enhance learning. Instead of telling the male trainee what he "should" do, the female field training officer might ask his opinion on a specific skill. For example, if his splinting skills need revision, she might ask, "What do you think about this procedure?"

These differences are merely the tip of a larger iceberg. In her book *He Says, She Says,* Lillian Glass identifies 105 differences in communication between men and women. These communication differences are divided into different categories, including body language, facial language, speech and voice patterns, and behavioral patterns. Below is a list of some of those differences in each area, followed by a suggestion on how the field training officer can overcome them.

Body Language

Men	Women
Take up more physical space	Take up less physical space
Use more forceful gestures	Use more fluid, easy, and light gestures
Gesture away from the body	Gesture toward the body
Tend to be in reclined positions	Tend to be in more forward positions
Use body language that gives less listener feedback	Use body language that gives more listener feedback
Invade another person's body space	Stay out of another person's body space
Touch others more often	Touch others less often
Fidget and change position more	Fidget and change position less

Overcoming some of these body language differences may include:

Men	Women
Using less gestures and keep gestures to the self	Expanding presence to take up more physical space, moving arms more
Not getting too close to the other person	Getting a little closer when necessary to make a point
Refraining from touching or use touch as a congratulatory response	Using touch appropriately, for example, as a congratulatory response

Facial Language

Men	Women
Avoid eye contact	Look more directly at another person
Look at another person at an angle	Face another person directly
Display frowning and squinting	Display smiling and head nodding
Use fewer facial expressions	Use more facial expressions
Stare more in negative interaction	Lower eyes to avert gaze

Overcoming some of these facial language differences may include:

Men	Women
Looking into another person's eyes	Maintaining eye contact, but do not stare
Using friendlier facial gestures, smiling	Smiling less during intense conversation
Being aware of staring during controversy	Looking at another person during controversy

Speech and Voice Patterns

Men	Women
Interrupt others more	Interrupt others less
Allow fewer interruptions	Allow more interruptions
Use more filler words (*uh, um*)	Use less filler words
Use sloppier pronunciation	Use quicker and more precise pronunciation
Use less intonation and vocal inflection	Use more intonation and vocal inflection
Use more monotonous speech	Sound more emotional

Men	Women
Speak louder	Speak in a softer voice
Use loudness to emphasize points	Use pitch and inflection for emphasis
Make direct accusations ("You don't . . .")	Make indirect accusations ("Why don't you . . .")
Are less verbose—get to the point	Are more verbose—slow to get to the point
Use more "command" terms	Use tones of politeness

Overcoming some of these speech and voice pattern differences may include:

Men	Women
Speaking quieter	Speaking more authoritatively
Watching for shouting when making point	Being specific when addressing a problem
	Being more concise

Behavioral Patterns

Men	Women
Have a more analytical approach	Have a more emotional approach
Give fewer compliments	Give more compliments
Are more task oriented ("What are you up to?")	Are more process oriented ("Is everyone OK?")
Are more assertive in communications	Are less assertive in communications
Are more argumentative	Are less argumentative
Tell more anecdotes and jokes	Tell less anecdotes and jokes
Hold fewer grudges	Hold more grudges
See time with beginning, middle, and end	See time as continuous flow
Are less likely to ask for help	Are more likely to ask and accept help
Are more blunt	Are more diplomatic

Overcoming some of these speech and voice pattern behavioral differences may include:

Men	Women
Giving more compliments	Being more analytical in approach
Reducing the tendency to argue	Getting to the point quicker
Being less anecdotal, telling fewer jokes	Forgeting grudges—when it's over, it's over
Asking for assistance when needed	

SUMMARY

Gender differences in the way we communicate can pose some problems for the field training officer when teaching an employee of the opposite gender. Being aware of the gender differences discussed in this chapter will facilitate communication between men and women. When a conflict does arise, they can redirect their efforts into being understood or understanding what the other person is saying.

7

Yes, I Really Hear You

Empathic Listening, Body Language, and Noise

How many times have you heard, "You don't understand" or "You're not listening to me?" How often have you been listening and wanting to talk? In his book *The 7 Habits of Highly Effective People,* Stephen Covey says that people listen not with the intent to understand, but with the intent to reply. People are either speaking or getting ready to speak, but they are not really listening to the other person. As Covey states, people tend to reply based on their own "home videos"—experiences in their own lives. Conversations become collective monologues, and people never really understand how the other person feels or perceives what is being said. This chapter will present another idea: empathic listening and how to use this form of listening to get to the emotional root of a conversation. It should be noted that the term *empathic listening* has often been used synonymously with *active listening,* a more commonly used phase.

In addition, this chapter will present information on how our body language can enhance or impede communication. As will be discussed, our body language plays a major role in our communication.

Finally, there are blocks to communication, most often called noise. This noise can be psychological or physical. This chapter will discuss how noise can interfere with communication between the field training officer and employee.

EMPATHIC LISTENING

When we are listening to someone else, we might be "listening" in one of four ways. We may be ignoring the speaker, pretending to listen ("Yeah, um-hmm"), practicing *selective listening* (hearing only what we want to hear), or practicing *attentive listening* (focusing on the words, not the feelings). There is a fifth level of communication that very few of us achieve. The fifth level is called *empathic listening*—understanding the other person's frame of reference. This can be especially helpful if the field training officer has been assigned a veteran employee who may be having difficulty performing the job. There could be any factors that are interfering with the employee's performance and, by empathically listening to the employee, the field training officer might be able to understand that the root of the problem could be a performance issue or a problem that is behavior oriented, based on outside-the-job influences. In either case, empathic listening could lead to expedited and successful remediation of the problem.

Communication experts estimate that only 7 to 10 percent of our communication comes from the words we use. But communication also comes from the sounds we make or how the words are said (30 to 38 percent) and the body language we use (55 to 60 percent). Empathic listening is developed by using all your senses, not just your ears, when listening to someone. You listen with your ears and your heart. When you fully understand the words and emotions of another person, you can then focus on the problem and come to a resolution. It is important to listen before:

- Making comments
- Adding to or making a counterpoint
- Evaluating or critiquing
- Providing information

Empathic listening involves techniques such as parroting the other person. But you are not merely repeating the other person's words. You are attempting to fully understand his or her view. For example, you can use phrases such as "What I just heard you say was . . ." or "You seem to be saying . . ." If you are not sure what the other person meant, be sure to ask for clarification. But do not use words that accuse or attempt to control (see "Blocks to Communications," below). In three words, empathic listening involves:

Listening—Carefully listen to the speaker, including verbal and nonverbal communication.

Identifying—Identify the speaker's emotions, including any experiences the person may have had that may have contributed to their feelings.

Responding—Let the speaker know your understanding of what he or she is saying and ask if your interpretation is correct.

Understanding the other person is only a part of the communication process. The other half is being understood by the other person. By clearly presenting your ideas, thoughts, or feelings, the other person will be better able to understand your frame of reference. If at any time during your communication you do not understand something, ask. This same concept should be explained to the employee, encouraging him or her to ask questions as they arise.

BODY LANGUAGE

Body language can enhance or detract from communication. Your posture, arm and leg positioning, facial expression, and activity during communication when talking with someone can invite the other person to tune in or tune out. Many times, the body language is so subtle that neither person is consciously aware of it. Subconsciously, however, each person is acutely aware of what the other is trying to "say" with their body.

Tune-In Body Language

Arms and legs open
- Arms unfolded or behind head, hands together (fingers together)
- Legs unfolded

Direct eye contact

Smiling

Leaning toward the person

Tune-Out Body Language

Arms and legs closed
Arms crossed, legs crossed
Fingers tapping on desk or table
Browsing through papers
Fidgeting with clothing or objects
Little, if any, eye contact
Frowning
Pulling away from other person
Ignoring behavior

If you notice an employee becoming quiet and, perhaps, distracted, consider what your body language is telling him or her. Make changes as appropriate.

BLOCKS TO COMMUNICATION

Noise—Physical or Psychological

"Noise" is defined as anything that hampers the effectiveness of communication. There are two types of "noise"—physical and psychological. Physical noise can be actual sounds, or it can be conditions that distract either the sender of the message, the receiver of the message, or both. Some examples of physical noise include a radio (dispatcher or music), construction activities, traffic sounds, temperature, and lighting. If there is anything in the area that hinders you or the other person's concentration, it is best to either remove the noise or go to another location.

Psychological noise refers to internal factors that hinder the sender's ability to express him- or herself or the receiver's ability to understand the message. An example of psychological noise is stress caused by something other than the immediate incident. If it appears that psychological noise is interfering with communication, it is best to discuss the internal noise and resolve it or delay the communications until the psychological distractor has been eliminated.

Another example of psychological noise is the perception that the conversation is an attack on the receiver. Communications can break down whenever one person perceives an attack and takes a defensive position. A confrontation in which talking (or yelling) is continuing, but no one is listening, is best avoided by not inviting the other person to become defensive. A defensive response is usually caused by using what is known as "controlling" behavior. The following is a list of controlling behaviors that can hinder effective communication:

Controlling space

Using elaborate arguments to wear someone down in a discussion
Invading privacy

Controlling with emotion

Sulking
Refusing to talk
Strutting and posturing
Grandstanding

Controlling someone else's reality

"That's not what you said/did."
"That's not what happened."
"That's not what you saw."
"That's not what you felt."

Controlling by defining someone's motivation

Telling someone why they did what they did, as if they knew

Controlling by making the other person responsible

"I did it because of you." "What's that doing there?"

Controlling by assigning status

Putting someone down
Putting someone up (used to get someone to do something they do not want to do)
Sentencing ("You are wrong to. . . .")
Categorizing ("All men/women. . . .")
Characterizing ("You are just like. . . .")

Other hindrances to effective communication are what are referred to as verbal abuse. Below are some examples of verbal abuse that invite the other person to become defensive:

Withholding	Countering
Discounting	Disguising a shot as a joke
Blocking	Accusing and blaming
Judging	Trivializing
Undermining	Threatening
Name calling	Forgetting
Ordering and demanding	Denial
Abusive anger	

How do you know someone is trying to control the communication? Unless you are astutely listening to what is being said, and how, controlling behavior could be difficult to recognize. However, if you are feeling uneasy or apprehensive when talking with a colleague or partner, investigate your feelings. Chances are the person could be attempting to control you.

Another Stumbling Block—Semantic Interference

Another block to effective communication is called semantic interference. Semantics is the study of meanings and, in semantic interference, there is a difference in understanding the meaning of a word or concept. For example, many common words have multiple definitions, and the understanding of those words may be different between two people who are talking.

Simplistically stated, semantic interference means that the person hearing the information or a specific word does not attribute the same meaning to the word as the person saying it. The use of jargon or job lingo is an example of semantic interference. If you are talking to a trainee and are discussing a new concept, it is important to use common words or phrases that have a clear meaning understood by most people. For example, most of us use jargon or slang at times. One trainee overheard a paramedic say, "We nuked the patient at 360." The trainee looked horrified and asked if the patient had been X-rayed or microwaved.

It is always important to ensure that the other person has understood what was discussed. To confirm that the message has been received correctly, ask the trainee to repeat the information in his or her own words.

SUMMARY

This chapter has discussed empathic listening, in which the field training officer can get to the emotions behind the communication. Actively listening to the employee means being involved in the communication and letting the employee know that he or she is being heard.

We also discuss how body language can play a key role in listening as well as speaking. With body language, the field training officer can subtly indicate that he or she is listening to or tuning out the employee.

Not only does body language play an important role in interpersonal communications, so does noise—both physical and psychological. While changing locations or modifying the environment can alter physical noise, reducing psychological noise takes considerably more effort. Further, some people may attempt to control communication by words or behaviors that can block an effective exchange of ideas.

Since the field training officer will most often be in a one-on-one setting with the trainee or employee, being aware of some of the intricacies of interpersonal communication can enhance the employee's training experience.

8

Games People Play

A major stumbling block to communication is the "game." A game, in this sense, is a "mind game" in which one person attempts to control another or invite feelings of inferiority in another. In 1964, Eric Berne published his now famous book *Games People Play,* which discusses psychological games that are used primarily to control or discount another person. According to Berne, a game has an ulterior motive with an ultimate payoff. Every game is basically dishonest, and every game has a dramatic quality. The purpose of this chapter is to identify some of the "games" that trainees may play against the field training officer or managers.

WHY PLAY GAMES?

The primary goal of the game is to invite the "victim" to feel badly about him- or herself; to invite negative feelings of self-worth in the victim; and to reinforce feelings of superiority in the game player. These games can be played against the field training officer at work to invite him or her to feel badly. There are several categories of games, including life games, marital games, party games, sexual games, underworld games, consulting room games, and good games. Because we are focusing on the role of the field training officer, we will only discuss games that can directly affect the field training officer's relationship with new and veteran employees.

NOW I'VE GOT YOU...

The intent of NIGYSOB is to set someone up for a fall and, when he or she fails, to chastise the person with full force. The aim is justification of anger against the other person, since the aggressor subconsciously resents the victim. The players in this game can be supervisors and employees, parents and children, or marital partners.

The setup involves giving the victim instructions that are only partially complete. The aggressor intentionally omits a very crucial step that will, ultimately, cause the victim to fail. When the victim does fail, the aggressor berates and discounts the victim. Unless the victim is aware of the game, he or she plays the role appropriately and feels badly about themselves. In order to stop the game, the victim must remain calm and analyze the situation. The victim must identify the aggressor's role in the victim's failure, especially if the instructions were incomplete.

WHY DON'T YOU . . . YES BUT (YDYB)

The intent of YDYB is to invite assistance from another person, but discount each option the victim suggests. Ultimately, the victim feels helpless, with a sense of failure. The aggressor asks for assistance with a problem. For each option the victim suggests, the aggressor replies with, "Yes, I could do that, but . . ." and gives an excuse for why that option will not work. After several suggestions, the aggressor tells the victim that maybe he or she cannot help and, perhaps, it was a mistake to ask the victim for help. The victim feels frustrated, and if the game is played right, useless. The players in this game can be supervisors and employees, parents and children, or marital partners.

You can stop the game by being acutely aware of the "Yes, but . . ." response. After the first "Yes, but . . ." you should listen carefully for the next one. Upon hearing the next "Yes, but . . ." you can stop the game by asking the aggressor what he or she would like to do about the problem.

WATER COOLER (WC)

Water cooler is a variation of a game called Ain't It Awful, which is exactly as it sounds—complaining. Actually, it is more of a pastime, since it does not have an ultimate payoff. Water cooler is generally played by two or more employees gathered around a common site, such as the water cooler. One of the employees begins to denounce a certain aspect of the company, the boss, a supervisor, a new policy, or some other aspect of the job. Other employees join in the conversation and grouse. The major problem with WC is that it can decrease employee morale, especially in employees who have little complaint with the company. The best way to reduce the incidence of this game is to not get involved, to stop the game by countering the initial negative comment.

LET'S YOU AND HIM FIGHT (LYAHF)

LYAHF is typically a game played in a romantic relationship; however, it can find its way into the business world rather easily. This game is a three-person game in which one person instigates an argument between two coworkers. Supervisors and employees have been known to play this game rather frequently.

Two employees are brought into the office. The supervisor looks at one employee and tells him that the other employee has said something bad about him. The supervisor then sits back and watches the fireworks. As the game advances, the supervisor will jump in and calm the dispute, inviting the other game players to view the supervisor as a problem solver. The supervisor is the aggressor in the game and wins the ultimate payoff. The best way to avoid this game is to use words that do not invoke resentment between coworkers who have a problem. Rather, invite and motivate the employees to resolve their own differences.

COURTROOM

A game that is related to LYAHF is Courtroom. Two employees who are having a dispute play this game. They bring their dispute to the supervisor, who is asked to make a decision. While on the surface the victim appears to be one of the battling employees, the real victim could, in fact, be the supervisor. To avoid being the victim, place the burden of finding the solution to the problem on the shoulders of each of the employees.

The examples given are some of the games you might encounter as a field training officer. Unfortunately, there are many other games that people can and do play against each other. If you are starting to feel resentful or frustrated in your conversation, investigate those feelings and determine if you are the unwitting player in a psychological game. If you think a game is being played, redirect the conversation to another topic or end it.

SUMMARY

This chapter has focused on psychological or mind games that can be played against the field training officer. Some employees may feel threatened by the trainer's position and want to make the field training officer feel or look bad among the other employees. By being aware of these games, the field training officer can refuse to play and stop the vicious process as soon as it begins.

COMMUNICATION—SECTION SUMMARY

This section, "Communication," has presented information on how people interact while sharing thoughts, feelings, knowledge, and more. As a field training officer, you will need to enhance your communication skills so that the new employee can benefit from your expertise. By knowing some of the ins and outs of effective communication and how to overcome stumbling blocks, the new employee will enjoy the benefit of having you show him or her "the ropes."

This section has presented information on transactional analysis, gender differences in communication, empathic listening, body language, blocks to communication, and mind games. The information discussed will assist the field training officer in better managing interpersonal communication.

Management

Although not directly involved in day-to-day management, the field training officer is part of management. Actually, the field training officer position is in limbo between the field and management. While the field training officer may or may not make management decisions, he or she will be privy to management information, policies, and direction. In a sense, the field training officer is part of the management team.

Because of the field training officer being a part of that management team, there will be times when he or she will function as a manager or supervisor. This section of the book is devoted to discussing some of the principles of management with which the field training officer should be familiar. It is not intended to be a full course on EMS management; however, the section will introduce the field training officer to managing employees.

9

Management

A Definition Dilemma

What is management? According to the dictionary, management is the "act or skill of controlling the movement or behavior; directing." This definition is lacking because it does not say anything about the finer principles of managing or supervising other people. Management is a bit of an art and science, but it mostly consists of people skills. The purpose of this chapter is to refine management's definition. Defining management is not easy, as there are a large number of ways to explain it. This chapter will highlight a couple of definitions.

WHAT IS MANAGEMENT?

Do the terms *managing* or *supervising* mean controlling or overseeing? Is a manager better defined as someone who leads, guides, or influences? There are a lot of ways of looking at the term *management*. Many employees look at management as a group of people who make decisions and set the policies and procedures for the organization. However, there is a bit more to management than setting policies and procedures.

Traditionally, management refers to the activities or people involved with planning, organizing resources of the agency, leading the employees, and controlling or coordinating the agency's systems, policies, procedures, and structures to enable the agency to meets its goals and objectives.

In planning, management often identifies goals and objectives, setting dates for task completion. In addition, managers may also be involved in strategic planning, such as identifying equipment and staffing needs for the near and foreseeable future.

Management is involved in organizing the resources of the agency, such as office staff, field staff, and office and field equipment. They frequently spearhead reorganization of the EMS agency.

Management is also responsible for leading. This may include setting the agency's direction, influencing decision makers such as politicians to agree to the direction management feels is best for the agency. Leading also includes creating mission and value statements and championing those statements to all of the agency's staff.

While one view of management holds that it is controlling in nature, another view consists of the concept that management's purpose is to support the employee and his or her efforts to be a productive member of the organization. Management is responsible for providing employees with the equipment, training, and support to do the work. Here is a better, single-sentence definition of management that was relayed by Paul Guglielmino, professor of business at Florida Atlantic University.

Management is the conscious, orderly, human approach of getting things done through others.

In managing others, you want to get them to do things for you and to initiate a spark that invites them to do a good job. There are essential components of management that are stated in the definition above. Understanding these components will make your job as a supervisor much more rewarding.

Conscious—You have to be aware of what you are doing. You cannot blindly go about giving orders, hoping that your orders will be carried out. You need to be aware of any changes that need to be made in the directions that you give.

Orderly—There needs to be a sequence or order to management. Crisis management has repeatedly been shown to be ineffective. Management needs to have goals and objectives, as well as measurements to see if the goals and objectives have been met.

Human—Effective managers realize they are dealing with people, not animals or machines. Each employee has human needs and wants, and a manager works with these needs and wants to achieve the employee's goals and the goals of the organization.

Along with the above definition is a corollary that enhances the overall concept of management.

Management is an athletic, moral, and intellectual activity; it is as much the product of the mind as of energy, determination, and integrity.

How do these definitions apply to the field training officer? The FTO needs to be fully aware of his or her role within the organization and give clear information to any trainee. When teaching, there are times when you might want to go on automatic mode and let your mind wander elsewhere. Errors can occur with the information that you are presenting, or you might miss important nonverbal clues from the trainee. Teaching also involves the orderly transfer of information—knowledge or skills—to the trainee. Skills are applied sequentially, not randomly, so order is important. Finally, as a field training officer, you need to be cognizant of the trainee's human nature. Not everyone learns at the same rate, and not everyone can perform a skill at peak proficiency. There may be outside influences that are blocking communication and affecting learning.

Teaching takes energy, is intellectual, and involves integrity. When you teach a class that lasts for several hours, there is an energy drain that you feel at the end of the session. You are spending your time and energy tapping into your knowledge to share it with others. Finally, you, as an educator, must act with integrity. There can be no favorites and no unfair biases, even if a trainee is your best friend. It is extremely difficult to retract a breach of integrity.

Your Place in the Organization

So, where do you fit within the management hierarchy of your organization? Refer to your agency's organizational chart and identify your place as well as your line of supervision. Who do you report to and to whom does your manager report? If you are the head of your agency's training section, chances are you are on a similar level as the chief of operations. If you are a field trainer, you may be aligned with shift commander, captain, or lieutenant. Although your scope of management may be narrow, you could be responsible for managing those individuals in a training environment.

YOUR MANAGEMENT ATTITUDE

How Do You Feel About Managing People?

Managers have certain attitudes and beliefs about supervising and leading others. To get a sense of the attitudes of entry-level and experienced managers, take a look at the management attitudes quiz below. Read the statements and indicate whether you agree or disagree with them. After completing and scoring the quiz, continue reading to interpret your score.

MANAGEMENT ATTITUDES

Read each statement carefully. For each statement, indicate whether you (1) Strongly Agree, (2) Agree, (3) Undecided (4) Disagree, or (5) Strongly Disagree.

1.	It soon becomes unpleasant to work for people who are very concerned with planning for productivity and efficiency.	1	2	3	4	5
2.	If I expect a high level of performance from my field personnel, I am sure to get a lot of griping and back talk.	1	2	3	4	5
3.	My field personnel work best when I leave them alone to do the job they know needs to be done.	1	2	3	4	5
4.	A good job must take time. If I try to speed things up, the quality of the work will suffer.	1	2	3	4	5
5.	If I trust the field personnel to do their best, I don't need to find ways to continue checking on them.	1	2	3	4	5
6.	It isn't essential for supervisors to hold their field personnel to definite standards.	1	2	3	4	5
7.	If one of my employees takes longer to do a job than I expected, the best thing to do is ignore the situation as long as it doesn't happen often.	1	2	3	4	5
8.	If I start trying to change the way field personnel do their jobs, I am likely to create more problems than I solve.	1	2	3	4	5
9.	When I assign a job to a particular person, it is not necessary to make it clear that I expect the job done in a certain period of time.	1	2	3	4	5
10.	Morale in our organization won't last if the field personnel think their jobs depend on working harder.	1	2	3	4	5
11.	In supervising field personnel, it is very important to avoid confrontations; either I accept them as they are or get rid of them.	1	2	3	4	5
12.	I can try to make field personnel more productive, but the quality of their work will suffer.	1	2	3	4	5
13.	In my agency, I can't expect to change things very much.	1	2	3	4	5

14. New supervisors may think they are going to make a big hit by holding their personnel to high standards, but they soon learn that doing so does not work.	1	2	3	4	5
15. Lots of field personnel have no intent in doing anything on the job except collecting their pay.	1	2	3	4	5
16. I expect my employees to be absent from work sometimes. I don't think I have to talk to them about why they were absent when they return.	1	2	3	4	5
17. If my field personnel find out they can influence my decisions, they will start complaining about everything under the sun.	1	2	3	4	5
18. It usually makes no difference in my employees' productivity if I remind them of goals.	1	2	3	4	5
19. I expect the field personnel I supervise to do a good job. I don't believe in praising them just because they do.	1	2	3	4	5
20. It is only natural for employees to want to earn as much money as possible for as little work as possible.	1	2	3	4	5
21. Many field employees like to grumble, but as long as they keep on working and don't bother me, I say, let them grumble.	1	2	3	4	5
22. Field personnel do a better job when they are a little afraid of their supervisors.	1	2	3	4	5
23. Most transportation service personnel work for money, not because they take pride in doing a good job.	1	2	3	4	5
24. The way people work is a result of their nature, and a supervisor cannot do much about that.	1	2	3	4	5
25. It is best to assume that field personnel work only because they have to and not because they like to work.	1	2	3	4	5
26. The best field personnel do not need supervision or instruction. They know what needs to be done and they will do it.	1	2	3	4	5
27. A group of employees gets along best when each person minds his or her own business.	1	2	3	4	5
28. The only way to lower turnover among field personnel is to hire better employees.	1	2	3	4	5
29. It is usually best for a supervisor to explain what needs to be done—not why it has to be done.	1	2	3	4	5
30. Many managerial problems would disappear if the supervisors just fired the workers who do not produce.	1	2	3	4	5

Continue to the next page for scoring.

Scoring the Management Attitude Self-Assessment

The statements on the self-assessment test are grouped into specific categories. For each group of statements, add the point scores for each statement and place the total in the space provided.

Group 1—Statements 3, 5, 7, 11, 12, 16, 19, 26, 29	Total points: _______
Group 2—Statements 4, 8, 13, 17, 21, 24, 27, 28, 30	Total points: _______
Group 3—Statements 1, 2, 6, 9, 14, 18	Total points: _______
Group 4—Statements 10, 15, 20, 22, 23, 25	Total points: _______

After totaling the points for each group, label the bar graphs by drawing a line with your position and compare your management attitudes with those entry-level and experienced managers.

Group 1 These statements indicate whether your style of management is **passive** or **active.** Active management style is rewarding, instructing, correcting, stating expectations, and following up on instructions. A passive style of management is more of a hands-off style.

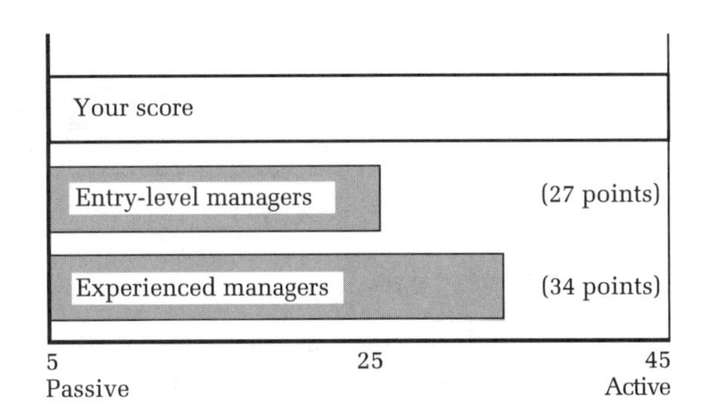

Group 2 These statements indicate whether you are **pessimistic** or **optimistic** about producing change, making decisions, motivating others, communicating clearly, and teaching others.

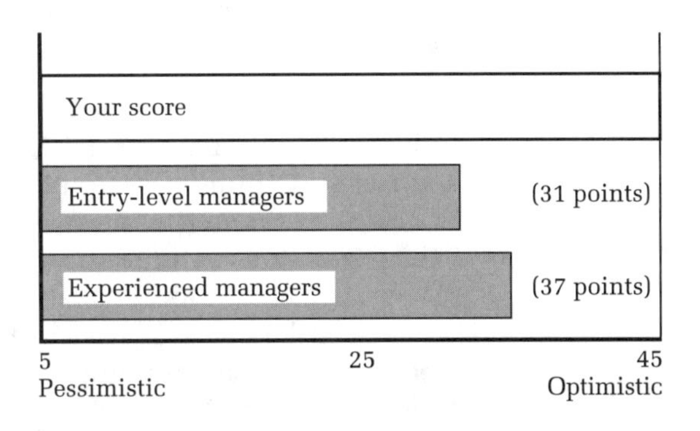

Group 3 These statements indicate whether you believe that setting goals and standards for your employees is **unimportant** or **important.**

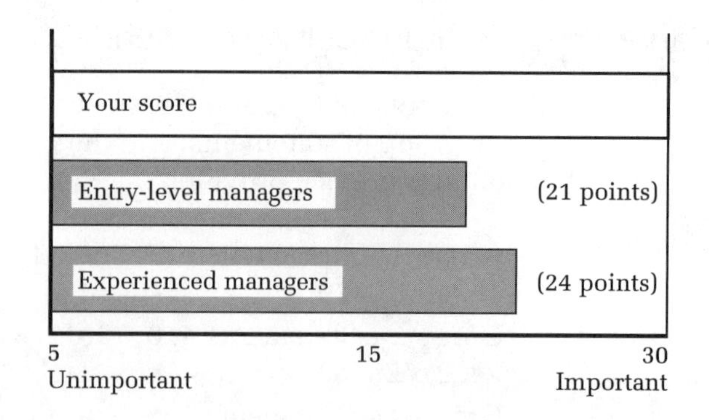

Group 4 These statements tell whether you feel an employee's source of motivation is **extrinsic** (coming from stimulation outside the employee, such as pay, fear, and authority) or **intrinsic** (coming from within the person, such as pride, self-esteem, and desire to succeed).

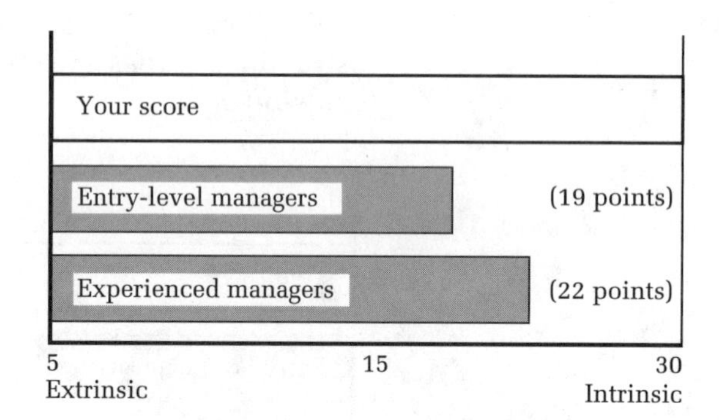

In looking at your scores, compare them with those of entry-level and experienced managers. If your scores are the same or higher than those scores, you have good attitudes about management and supervision. If your scores are below those of entry-level managers, carefully examine each group of statements to see where you can make changes in your management beliefs.

THEORY X VERSUS THEORY Y

Among the many different management theories is one that contrasts what is known as Theory X and Theory Y. In the 1950s, Professor Douglas McGregor at the Massachusetts Institute of Technology observed that neither cash, working conditions, nor punishment worked as a continuing incentive for employees. McGregor theorized that attitudes toward and treatment of employees could influence job performance. McGregor came up with two different management styles, Theory X and Theory Y, based upon their treatment of the employees. McGregor believed that greater employee fulfillment and managerial satisfaction was based on Theory Y.

Below is a table discussing the basic beliefs in each of the two management theories.

Theory X	Theory Y
The emergency medical services employee, like most people, has an inherent dislike for work and will avoid it if possible.	The expenditure of physical and mental effort in work is as natural as in play or rest. The employee does not inherently dislike work.
EMS agency employees need to be coerced, controlled, service directed, and threatened with punishment to perform quality work.	External control and threat are not the only ways to get emergency medical employees to perform quality work.
Emergency medical services employees prefer to be directed, want to avoid responsibility, have relatively little ambition, and want security most of all.	The average emergency medical services employee learns, under the right conditions, not only to accept, but to seek, responsibility.
	Most EMS agency employees have the capacity to exercise a relatively high degree of imagination, integrity, and creativity in the solution of problems found within the agency.

Management experts have debated the pros and cons of each theory and have determined that some aspects of each theory work well with different employees. Some employees work better under Theory X, while others produce better results under Theory Y. Depending on the employee, you might need to adopt some principles from each theory to get the desired results. For example, if you recognize that your trainee is a self-starter, you may not have to give detailed instructions for reviewing or studying specific topics. That employee is motivated and needs no coercion. In contrast, there are some trainees that need to be led by the hand through each session. Coaxing and cajoling the employee may be needed to get him or her through the training session.

SUMMARY

Because the field training officer is in a gray area between the field staff and management, this chapter presented basic information about management—its structure and some underlying theories. It assessed your managerial attitudes, allowing you to see where you stand in relation to entry-level and experienced managers. As mentioned at the beginning, this chapter is not a comprehensive discussion about managing employees. Rather, it gives you some insight into the structure and function of middle- and senior-level managers.

In the chapters that follow, the book will address leadership as well as give you some tips on working with employees, using your position as a field training officer effectively.

10

Leadership

The field training officer will also be in a leadership position. This role can be challenging to the field training officer because leadership is difficult, and, depending on the circumstances, it might have to be changed or modified. You may ask, "How is an FTO a leader? Don't we rely upon the managers for leadership?" Not necessarily. One comparison holds that leaders do the right thing, while managers do things right. As you can see, the concept of leadership is confusing. The purpose of this chapter is to reduce the confusion over the term *leadership,* identify the types of leaders, and determine your leadership style.

LEADERSHIP AND POWER

There are a variety of leadership functions, all of which depend upon the leader's basis of power or influence. There are six categories of power. Most of these are intertwined or linked and can be mentioned together. The first two types of power are expert and informational power. This type of power is linked to knowledge, information, and skills that the leader can use to influence others. This is one of the key powers for a field training officer—having the skills, knowledge, and information that can be effectively used to teach others.

Two other categories of power include reward and coercive power. This involves the ability to reward or punish the individuals under your influence. This power is more often given to shift and top-level managers, and not typically found among field training officers.

The final two categories of power include legitimate power and referent power. Legitimate power is the degree of influence given to a person by his or her title of position within the organization. By its very title, the position of chief holds a lot of legitimate power. Referent power means that the person being influenced identifies in some form with the leader. This is most often seen with well-known celebrities who use their referent power in politics or for charitable causes. The field training officer may have a little legitimate power, but virtually no referent power.

LEADERSHIP TYPES

In addition to power, there are three basic leadership types that can be adopted by the field training officer to enhance learning and compliance with company rules and regulations. These leadership styles include the authoritarian, democratic, and laissez faire types.

The authoritarian leader directs subordinates in the tasks they are to perform, using legitimate powers, reward, and coercive powers to achieve goals. There is generally no room for disagreement. This style might be necessary in a critical emergency when time is important. Unfortunately, working under a continuous authoritarian leader can be stressful. Since there is no room for personal growth, employees can become resentful of the "dictator." The authoritarian FTO often encounters resistance when teaching others.

A second style of leadership is the democratic style: everyone in a work group has a say in the operations of the company. The leader solicits input and, after a vote is taken, a policy or procedure is either implemented or changed. In the field, the field training officer can ask about a procedure or invite the new employee's participation in patient care. A drawback to the democratic style is that the decision may get bogged down in "committee."

Trainees under the democratic style are generally more participative and productive. Personal growth and taking responsibility in their training and learning is a benefit to this style. However, "managing by committee" has its drawbacks. Arguments, although infrequent, over the best way to proceed or the effects of a new policy could stagnate the process. Here, expert and informational power is most often used to influence the group or trainee. Even with all the input from others, the field training officer has to make the ultimate decision as it pertains to a particular event or situation.

"Remember that mouth-to-mouth technique you've been dying to show me?"

Laissez faire, or hands-off, is the third style of leadership. Since there is no direction by the manager or supervisor, the employees have to deal with things on their own. While this is good for highly motivated self-starters, it may not work well with all employees. This style of leadership can result in low achievement or productivity if not tempered with authoritarian and democratic styles.

SELF-ASSESSMENT

So, what kind of leader are you? Are you a hands-off or dictatorial leader? Are you a team player or one that has no clue? A tool for assessing managerial style is the Blake–Moulton Managerial Grid, which assesses the degree of your concern for tasks or production versus your concern for people. It will assess your leadership style and let you know if your style is, at the extremes, "Authoritarian," "Country Club," or somewhere in between. Complete the Blake–Moulton Managerial Grid below and then plot your score on the grid that follows to determine your leadership style.

Blake–Moulton Leadership Styles

Read each of the statements below carefully. Using the scale below, indicate how the statement pertains to you.

Scale

Never		Sometimes			Always
0	1	2	3	4	5

1. _______ I encourage my team to participate when decision-making time arrives, and I try to implement their ideas and suggestions.
2. _______ Nothing is more important than accomplishing a goal or task.
3. _______ I closely monitor the schedule to ensure a task or project will be completed on time.
4. _______ I enjoy coaching people on new tasks and procedures.
5. _______ The more challenging a task is, the more I enjoy it.
6. _______ I encourage my employees to be creative about their job.
7. _______ When seeing a complex task through to completion, I ensure that every detail is accounted for.
8. _______ I find it easy to carry out several complicated tasks at the same time.
9. _______ I enjoy reading articles, books, and journals about training, leadership, and psychology, and then putting what I have read into action.
10. _______ When correcting mistakes, I do not worry about jeopardizing relationships.
11. _______ I manage my time very efficiently.
12. _______ I enjoy explaining the intricacies and details of a complex task or project to my employees.
13. _______ Breaking large projects into small manageable tasks is second nature to me.
14. _______ Nothing is more important than building a great team.
15. _______ I enjoy analyzing problems.
16. _______ I honor other people's boundaries.
17. _______ Counseling my employees to improve their performance or behavior is second nature to me.
18. _______ I enjoy reading articles, books, and trade journals about my profession, and then implementing the procedures I have learned.

Scoring: Put the number of points into the spaces by each statement number. Add each column and then multiply by 0.2 to get your final score for that column. After calculating your final score, plot it on the graph that follows.

People	Production
1.________	2.________
4.________	3.________
6.________	5.________
9.________	7.________
10.________	8.________
12.________	11.________
14.________	13.________
16.________	15.________
17.________	18.________

Total________ Total________
× 0.2________ (multiply times 0.2) × 0.2________ (multiply times 0.2)
Score________ Score________

Plot your score on the grid below.
Plot your assessment on the grid below to determine your managerial style.

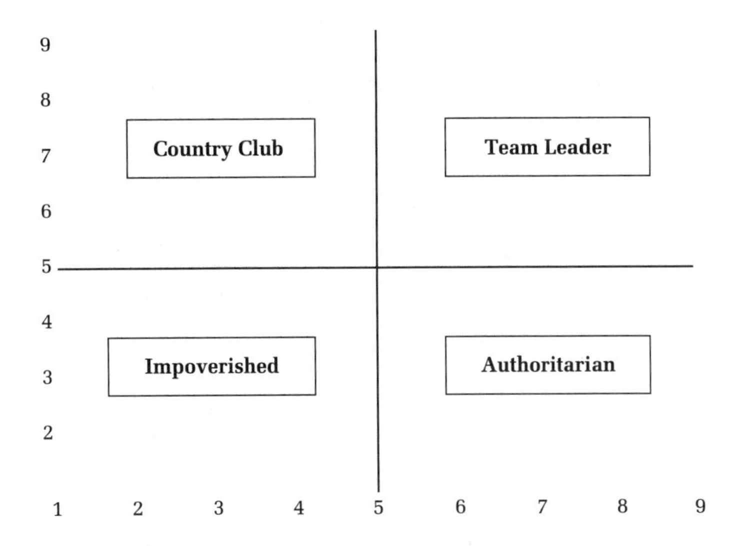

The leadership style has five strategic points, as described below:

Points	Assessment
1,1	Impoverished, or Hope-No-One-Is-Looking, style operates at a minimum level.
1,9	Country Club level favors people to the near exclusion of production.
9,1	Authoritarian is bent on production without concern for people.
5,5	Medium is balanced between the two, but compromises on each.
9,9	Team Leader, or Superstar, has things together and is the top leader.

This chart is not an end-all in managerial styles, but merely a tool to assess your style. The grid is based on your leadership emphasis, not necessarily how you actually perform the job. If you do not like the results, use the information as a stepping-off point to improve your style.

The FTO can have any one of the leadership styles. Consider the following examples:

Impoverished FTO—"That skill? Oh, yeah, however is OK with me."

Country Club FTO—Eventually the trainee will "get" the skill. Let him or her work on it for a while.

Authoritarian FTO—"Do it my way or else!"

Team Player FTO—Gets the trainee actively involved with the learning process and coaches effectively. Is focused on getting the skill done and the effect that a good job has on the trainee.

SUMMARY

This chapter presented information on being a leader. While a manager may also be a leader, a manager does not always possess leadership qualities. Being a leader involves a degree of power or influence. As a field training officer, your power is based on knowledge and information. So, in your position, you have the potential of being a leader of the employees.

In addition, this chapter talked about leadership styles and assessed your style through the Blake–Moulton survey. From your results on the survey, you can identify your leadership style and, if necessary, make changes to best accomplish your training goals and objectives.

11

Hints for Working with Others

In Chapters 9 and 10, this book has presented ideas about management and leadership, but it did not give you specific hints on how to work with fellow employees in a quasi-management or training role. This chapter will present ideas for you to consider as you develop in your role as a field training officer.

COUNSELING

There are various terms that can be used to describe a counseling session. Words such as interview, talk, meeting, or conversation imply an air of confidentiality and openness in which judgment of the person is absent and the focus of the meeting is on the employee's problem. Counseling consists of a one-on-one conversation between a supervisor and an employee to help the employee cope with problems that are upsetting to the employee. While employees with such problems will not usually be referred to "training," quite often an underlying problem manifests itself in a decrease in performance. That drop in performance can invite a referral to training for skill evaluation.

As a field training officer, you might see an employee who has been referred to training for poor performance and might uncover a counseling need. There may be other situations when your partner shows signs of emotional upset and, due to a close working relationship, may ask for your advice. Should this happen, be sure to refer the employee to the correct source for assistance. Thus, this section of the chapter is aimed at a high-level discussion about the procedures commonly used when counseling an employee.

Counseling will help when an employee's will to work or performance is marred by emotional upsets caused by a problem either on or off the job. Problems that can affect work performance include:

- Drug or alcohol abuse
- Conflict with other employees
- Health matters
- Finances
- Family difficulties

The need for counseling is usually apparent by changes in the employee's behavior. These changes might include:

- Mood changes: The employee is not acting in his or her usual way.
- Performance drop: The employee's work quality becomes unsatisfactory.

- Irritability: A cooperative person becomes easily quarrelsome or irritable.
- Fatigue: The employee becomes easily tired without an obvious physical cause.
- Accident proneness: A careful worker has a series of accidents.
- Touchiness: The employee suddenly resents criticism or suggestions.
- Troublemaking: The employee causes trouble or interferes with the work of others.

To be effective in counseling employees, you need to watch for or be alert to any of the above signals. Many times the need for counseling is brought to your attention by another employee; however, there will be times when the employee will ask for assistance. Whenever counseling is needed, there are several techniques you should use. Below are guidelines that will enhance the counseling session:

- Show courtesy, attention, patience, and sincerity.
- Promise confidentiality and maintain it. Breaching confidentiality undermines any trust the employee may have in you.
- Let the employee set the pace, but ask questions for clarification.
- Pinpoint the problem. Get to the root of it. This might require brainstorming where all of the possible causes are identified. If you meet resistance, stop and let the employee continue at his or her own pace. It might be necessary to continue the meeting at a later date.
- Get the employee's acceptance. If there is the need for a temporary reassignment, make sure the employee knows the reasons behind the reassignment and agrees to it. Also, get the employee's consent for follow-up. If another meeting or an appointment with a specialist is needed, make sure the employee agrees to the other meeting or appointment.
- Do not take on the employee's burden. Do not offer to help resolve the problem. The problem belongs to the employee. Offer understanding or resources that can be useful.
- Do not give advice, especially in financial or medical areas.
- Do not offer opinions or make judgments on the employee's ethics, morals, values, or actions. Encourage the employee to help in the decision-making process.

After completing the counseling session, write some notes about the meeting for future reference. In most cases, these notes do not need to go into the employee's personnel file. Rather, store them in a confidential and secure area so that you can refer to them during a follow-up.

CRITIQUING

The word criticism has, for many, negative connotations. It is seen as a put-down, discouragement, and a detriment to enthusiasm. The word *critique,* in contrast, is described as controlled criticism and is a systematic approach to spotting weakness, flaws, errors, and mistakes. Critiquing is useful in all areas of management and can remedy problems that are continuing or repetitive, either in a group meeting or in a one-on-one basis. There are several steps to effective critiquing.

As in counseling, first pinpoint the problem and carefully identify its root. If the problem is a company-wide issue, use brainstorming with other employees.

Once the problem has been clearly identified, determine what actions are necessary to resolve it. Again, brainstorming can be effective in listing all of the options available. After listing the options that can solve the problem, eliminate those that are not viable—those that are contrary to company policy or might be unlawful. Finally, decide upon a course of action and implement it, following through with an evaluation of the effectiveness of the action plan.

The same processes can be used with individual employees who have made errors or mistakes or those who have violated company policy. Be sure to completely identify and address the problem, not the person who committed the error. Second, refresh the employee in company policies and procedures, identifying steps that can be taken to correct the mistake. Make sure the employee understands the reasons for the correction and that he or she will make the necessary changes. Finally, follow up the employee's progress, reinforcing the positive change.

FRIENDSHIP

Being a Friend or Being Friendly

Friendship is a relationship that involves special feelings for a specific few people. In contrast, friendliness involves a warm and sympathetic attitude that can be shared with everyone. So, what is better—being a friend or being friendly?

The workplace fosters friendships. Many employees share similar interests and experiences, and "talking shop" is common at social functions. However, developing friendships at work can have pluses and minuses.

Being a friend of a coworker can pose problems, especially if you are perceived as being biased or unfair. At times, it might be necessary to tell your friend that you might have to go to some extremes not to seem biased against other employees. This can mean that your friend loses out on some things, straining your friendship.

Do not let your friendship interfere with your job duties. In management, you might be privileged to hear information not intended for anyone outside of management. Do not be tempted to let your friend "in" on company secrets.

Moving up the career ladder affects friendships. You have undoubtedly developed friendships with coworkers. Promotions tend to adversely affect these relationships. Your friends might think that you will give them special consideration or overlook minor infractions. When this does not happen, the friendship can wither and die. Be prepared for such changes. You may no longer be seen as "one of the troops." Rather, other employees might think of you as one of "them guys in management."

As friendships change and are no longer considered friendships, you can still be friendly with coworkers, treating them equally, fairly, and with respect. Sometimes it is a difficult choice—between remaining friends and being in management. For some, it is nearly impossible.

THOUGHTS FROM THE ONE-MINUTE MANAGER

Catch Them Doing Something Right

An excellent short, but powerful, management tool is the book *One-Minute Manager,* by Kevin Blanchard and Spencer Johnson. You can help an employee reach their full potential by giving them immediate feedback when they have done something good. According to Blanchard and Johnson, you can quickly praise a coworker and achieve tremendous results using their concept of **one-minute praising:**

In using these techniques, you want to:

- Tell people up-front that you are going to let them know how they are doing.
- Praise the employee immediately.
- Tell the employee what he or she did right and be specific.
- Tell the employee how good you feel about what they did right, but be sincere.
- Pause for a moment to let the employee feel how good you feel.
- Encourage them to keep up the good work.
- Shake hands or touch them in a way that lets them know of your support.

Unfortunately, there will be times when a reprimand is necessary. Like one-minute praising, there is a **one-minute reprimand,** which works best when you:

- Tell people up-front that you are going to let them know how they are doing.
- Reprimand them immediately but out of earshot of other employees.
- Tell the employee what he or she did wrong and be specific.
- Pause for a few seconds of uncomfortable silence.
- Shake hands with the employee or touch them to let them know you are on their side.
- Remind them of their value to you and the company.
- Reaffirm that you think well of them but not their performance in a particular situation.
- Recognize that when the reprimand is over, it is over. Employees resent reminders.

SUMMARY

This chapter has given you tips on effectively dealing with employees in your new role. Occasionally, as an FTO, you might find yourself in the role of a counselor—whether the employee approaches you directly or you see evidence that something is amiss in the employee's performance. This chapter also addresses a change in your relationship with your colleagues. Before, you may have been considered one of the gang and had established several friendships. In your new role, those friendships will change. Finally, use an effective technique from the *One-Minute Manager*—catch the employee doing something right. Using the tips presented here will make your job easier when you are viewed as a part of management and no longer one of the "field."

SECTION SUMMARY

This section has presented information about managing others. We have defined management, identified your management attitudes, discussed management Theory X and Theory Y, styles of leadership, and presented some hints on counseling and critiquing. By being an effective manager and leader, your responsibilities as a field training officer will be easier and more beneficial to the newly hired employee.

IV

On Being a Teacher

Teaching is more than standing up in front of a class and rambling about some subject. It takes work, preparation, and dedication. But it can also be a lot of fun.

Being a part of the educational process, or teaching, is rewarding. You can watch someone grow and mature in knowledge and abilities, knowing that you played a part in the process. Being a teacher, you influence the individual to achieve high standards, as well as provide a service to the employer.

There are several aspects of teaching and learning that are important for the field training officer. In order for a person to learn something, he or she must have access to the information and want to learn it. Second, the individual must be able to retain the information or be able to proficiently demonstrate the skill.

Before discussing the various aspects of education, you need to be familiar with some basic principles of learning and teaching. This section will address some of the fundamentals of learning, including memory as well as some theories on how we learn. It will also discuss how we process information—are we left- or right-brain dominant? Are we visual, auditory, or kinesthetic learners? Equally important is knowing about the adult learner and what he or she brings to the classroom. You may be surprised to learn that teaching adults is very different from teaching children.

After delving into some of the theories of how people learn and the nature of the adult learner, we will talk about teaching methologies for the field training officer. You will read about the various teaching techniques and learn the good and bad things about each technique. We will also discuss the tools of the educator's trade—slides, chalk or dry erase boards, and similar items. This section will present information about the types of trainees you will have—they are not all keenly attentive to the speaker.

Often, training is seen as the cure-all for what ails the EMS agency or, specifically, the employee. If you throw enough training at a problem, the problem will go away—wrong! Training often fails because the actual need has not been clearly established. The field training officer must perform a needs assessment and needs analysis on which to focus the training. Doing this means the field training officer needs to be a performance consultant, which is discussed in a later chapter in this section.

This section will get into the nitty-gritty of teaching—setting goals and objectives, developing a lesson plan, and constructing evaulation tools (tests) that will measure whether the employee learned the information.

Finally, this section will discuss developing a budget for training and give an example of the components of a budget along with an explanation of each component. The reader is also presented with a completed budget as an example of what one might look like.

12

Back to Basics

The Learning Process

In order for something to be learned, we must put that information into memory. Not only must we put it into memory, we must process it so that it has relevance to us. The purpose of this chapter is to discuss some of the basic principles of learning, including memory and the processes around learning new matieral. One of the fundamental rules of learning is:

I hear; I forget.
I see; I remember.
I do; I understand.

Simply stated, hearing something is not enough. People need to see it and, for hands-on skills, the student needs to perform it. It is important to remember that most of what people hear in a lecture will soon be forgotten. It is estimated that, in only hearing the information, 70 percent of what is heard is soon lost. To enhance learning, the student must see the information. Seeing the information in audiovisual presentations such as slides, overhead transparencies, or chalkboard presentation significantly increases retention. Similarly, watching a skill being performed enhances learning. Unfortunately, 30 percent of what is seen is soon forgotten. However, if the student participates in an activity related to the subject, he or she will retain up to 90 percent or more of the information. Not only will he or she remember the information, the student will also comprehend it and be able to use it later. But the key to learning something is putting the information into memory.

MEMORY—THE SHORT AND LONG OF IT

We are constantly bombarded with information. Each of our senses receives stimulation from something we see, hear, touch, smell, or taste. Do we remember all of the information we receive? No, because most of it is ignored. But how do we remember things such as information for a test or a skill? Most EMS instructors will agree—practice reinforces learning the information or skill. Yet learning does involve remembering, and memory is an important aspect to learning. The purpose of this section is to discuss two basic theories of memory and how people learn and retain information.

In 1968, Atkinson, R. L. and Shiffrin, R. M. proposed that there are three different types of memory—sensory memory, short-term memory, and long-term memory. Each play a part in our learning. Throughout the day, we are subject to continual stimulation of the senses. Information received by the senses is sent into sensory memory, where most of the input is ignored. However, if attention is paid to the information, it is sent to short-term memory.

Short-term memory can hold only a small amount of information for a short amount of time. Short-term memory can maintain seven "chunks" of information (plus or minus two), and, if not attended to or rehearsed, the information can be retained and recalled for approximately eighteen to twenty seconds. To illustrate this concept, consider a phone number. A phone number consists of seven digits. Each digit or series of digits can represent one chunk. After looking up the number in the telephone directory, it is rehearsed and remembered as it is dialed. Moments after the number is dialed, it is no longer attended to and promptly forgotten. If the area code is added to the telephone number, it becomes increasingly difficult to recall the information prior to or while dialing. But in some cases, the area code can form a single chunk of information. Thus, the seven-digit number plus the area code can be eight chunks of information. To further exemplify this chunking, a person may combine pairs of digits to enhance retention and recall. The last four numbers might be 1711, which are then chunked to 17 and 11. Thus, chunking can make room for additional information, such as the area code.

Another factor affecting short term memory is the primacy–recency effect. This means that when reviewing a list of items, the probability of recall is higher for items at the beginning of the list (primacy effect) and the end of the list (recency effect).

Short-term memory has also been called working memory. In working memory, information is kept alive by active rehearsal. Think about the phone number example above. As long as the number is replayed mentally, it can be recalled. In addition, the likelihood of the telephone number being transferred into long-term memory is increased. Again, if the information is not rehearsed or maintained, it will be deleted from short-term or working memory within a few seconds. The picture below illustrates the different areas of memory—sensory, short-term, and long-term memory.

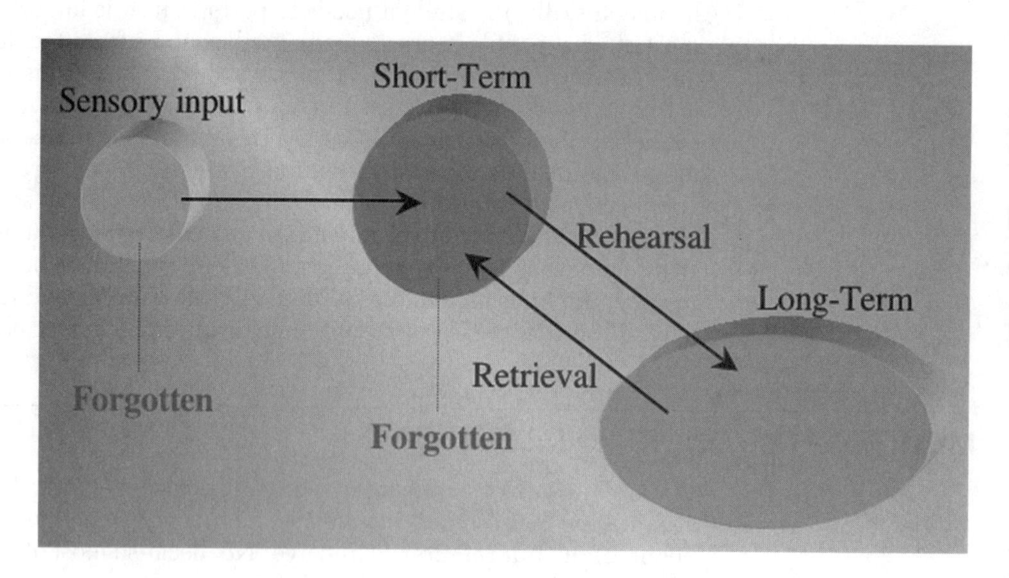

Working memory is used to rehearse, elaborate, and organize information so that it can be stored into long-term memory. During this rehearsal, strategies are developed to ensure storage into long-term memory. We organize the information by:

- Developing mnemonics
- Clustering or chunking the information

- Creating visual images
- Putting information into schemas (clusters based on prior experience)
- Developing scripts to organize knowledge about common things

The more elaborate the rehearsal and organization, the easier it is to transfer the information into long-term memory. In addition, the more elaborate and organized the rehearsal, the easier it is to recall the information when needed. Finally, links to old information are created that also facilitate storage. Once the rehearsal is complete, the information is stored in long-term memory. Unlike short-term memory, which has a time and storage limit, long-term memory is considered relatively permanent and limitless.

How is long-term memory created? Long-term memory is created by changes in the brain's "wiring" or in the conduction of impulses through the brain's synapses. In creating long-term memory, new connections are created while older ones are destroyed. There are a few theories on how these connections are created. One holds that there are biochemical changes in the brain that begin with learning. These reactions, which include the formation of new proteins, are responsible for connecting nerve cells that serve to create permanent memories. Damage to these proteins may be responsible for memory loss.

Recent discoveries, however, show evidence that the brain repeatedly replays a cellular event that eventually leads to cell connections and long-term memory. Some of these theories suggest that incomplete or erroneous memories are caused by an error in replaying the cellular event.

Researchers Fergus Craik and Robert Lockhart developed a different theory of memory. Their theory, called Levels of Processing, holds that memory is dependent on the depth of processing of specific information. Basically, the more meaning a person applies to the information, the deeper the processing. Their theory further suggests that the more meaning applied to the information, the stronger the connection in the brain and the easier the information is to recall. This is particularly true when considering the self-reference effect. This effect says that people apply more meaning to something when they can relate it to the self and can retrieve the information from memory more readily.

Once the information has been stored, it needs to be retrieved. Recognition and recall of the information characterize retrieval. To enable retrieval, we use cues and associations that trigger recall of the information. Cues are stimuli that aid in memory recall. Associations are categories and networks, or links, to specific information. For example, consider the brain as a huge filing cabinet. To locate a file we need to use a cue such as a topic or other hint as to where the file is located. Similarly, we need an association or link to previously stored data.

To give you an example of these associations, consider advertising jingles or phrases. Read the information in the left-hand column and see what memory it triggers. Compare your thoughts with the list in the right-hand column.

Plop, plop, fizz, fizz . . .	Oh, what a relief it is—Alka Seltzer
1-800- . . .	Call-ATT or COLLECT
Like a rock . . .	Chevy trucks
I can't believe I ate the whole thing.	You ate it, Ralph—Alka Seltzer
It's the real thing.	Coca-Cola
Must-see TV	NBC

Try another exercise. Think about a favorite song. Why did you recall that song? Was it the music or lyrics that caused it to transfer into long-term memory? Why was the song retrieved at this time? The most likely reason for the immediate recall is that the song had, at some point, intense meaning. How did you recall the information? What triggered the memories? Associations that were formed in the brain linked the words to other words or visual images so that recall was facilitated.

The nature of the above retrieval is based on contextual cues—giving basic information (hints) to allow links to memories. Contextual cues allow for the easiest recall. These kinds of cues are found in multiple choice test questions where the answer is somewhere within the distractors. Test questions that call for complete answers are the most difficult since there are no cues to the answer. Instead of relying upon the cues in possible answers, the student has to use schemas or clusters of knowledge taken from prior experience with the information in order to answer the question correctly.

After the student spends time reading and reviewing the information presented in class, does he or she really know the material? At a minimal level, probably. But at a higher level where the student can put the information into "action," there is a lot of work remaining.

CONCEPTS OF LEARNING

Putting information into memory is a part of learning, but there is a lot more to learning than memorization. Most training officers are well acquainted with the EMT or paramedic who can recite a textbook yet cannot perform tasks in the field. Besides memorization, the student also needs to process the information and assign a personal value to the material. Once the information has been processed, the student can incorporate the learned information into skills that he or she can effectively use. Thus, there are additional steps to the learning process that have been studied and analyzed in various theories of learning.

While there are a number of theories on learning (approximately fifty), one of the more popular that has endured continual review is known as Bloom's Taxonomy. This theory is easily understood and one of the more widely applied theories in education. Heading up a committee of colleges, Benjamin Bloom recognized that there are three areas of learning. These areas, called domains, have been labeled cognitive, affective, and psychomotor. In "noneducationalese," these terms mean "knowledge" (cognitive), "attitude" (affective), and "skills" (psychomotor). Within each domain are several categories that explain the learning processes. The categories are listed sequentially according to their degrees of difficulty. A student must achieve and master one category or level before proceeding to the next one.

Cognitive Domain (Knowledge)

The cognitive domain pertains to basic knowledge and intellectual development. It ranges from obtaining basic knowledge to evaluating the information and making a judgment regarding the information's value. It is important to note that the value is based on the student's perception of the material, not the instructor's value. Below is the hierarchy of categories within the cognitive domain, along with a basic description of that category. To help clarify the category, associated behaviors are listed in each section:

- **Knowledge:** Memorizing and recalling basic facts, definitions, signs, and symptoms.
  Behaviors: Define, identify, list, label, state, indicate, recite, show.
- **Comprehension:** Understanding the information enough to put into own words.
  Behaviors: Apply, classify, find, operate, summarize, describe.
- **Application:** Applying to the job and what the student is asked to do.
  Behaviors: Determine, chart, solve, use, develop, prepare.

- **Analysis:** Making comparisons and testing the validity of the information.
  Behaviors: Differentiate, compare, illustrate, relate, contrast.
- **Synthesis:** Putting the information together to use it in problem solving.
  Behaviors: Plan, organize, categorize, compose, revise, rewrite, summarize.
- **Evaluation:** Determining a value system and developing informed opinions.
  Behaviors: Critique, evaluate, judge, defend, justify, conclude.

Affective Domain (Attitude)

The affective domain involves assigning emotions, attitudes, and values to the information and learning. In a word, it is how the student "feels" about the learning—motivated, enthusiastic, appreciative. Like the cognitive domain, there are categories or levels the student will achieve. The five categories of the affective domain are listed below, along with key behaviors for each category:

- **Receiving:** Being aware of the importance of learning and listening attentively. Showing respect.
  Behaviors: Observe, attend, describe, follow, name, identify.
- **Responding:** Actively participating in and enjoying the class.
  Behaviors: Volunteer, answer, assist, help, perform, practice, reports, discuss.
- **Valuing:** Perceiving that something (behavior or object) has value or worth.
  Behaviors: Appreciate, differentiate, justify, invite, share, join, demonstrate.
- **Organizing:** Prioritizing values and resolving conflicts between values to form a consistent value system.
  Behaviors: Explain, defend, alter, formulate, integrate, modify, compare, synthesize.
- **Characterizing:** Internalizing values and acting accordingly. Exercising self-reliance when working on own.
  Behaviors: Act, practice, perform, display, qualify, question, solve, verify.

Psychomotor Domain (Skill)

A third domain involves learning and performing skills and requires movement and coordination. Since prehospital care is skill oriented, being able to make the brain–hand connection is important. There are five categories or levels in the psychomotor domain that are listed and described below. Key behaviors for each category are also listed for each level:

- **Imitation:** Imitating what the student sees the instructor perform. Skill quality is low.
  Behaviors: Copy, describe, duplicate.
- **Manipulation:** Adapting the skill and performing in own way. Mistakes are common.
  Behaviors: Create, demonstrate, show.
- **Precision:** Refining the skill and reducing errors. Practices the skill until precision is developed.
  Behaviors: Refine, rework, perform, create, explain, repeat.
- **Articulation:** Integrating new skill with others to form a complex skill.
  Behaviors: Produce, combine, coordinate.

- **Naturalization:** A skill that once started out as crude becomes natural. Knowing what to do and when to do it.
  Behaviors: Proficient, automatic, effective.

SUMMARY

This chapter presented information about some of the basic concepts behind learning—memory and processing information so that we can use it later. Almost everyone is familiar with short-term memory, but the real key to learning is putting the information into long-term memory, where it can be recalled when needed. In addition, this chapter talked about some of the processes identified by Bloom and his colleagues regarding how we process information. In order for the field training officer to be most effective, he or she must understand how memory works and the processes of turning important information into something we can use.

13

Learning Styles

It's Unique to You

As mentioned earlier in the previous chapter, estimates suggest that students forget 70 percent of what they hear. The odds of retention are better when seeing something, and are best when a student "experiences" a topic or task. However, these statements are not true for everyone or in every situation. People learn differently. Focusing on one learning style to the exclusion of others is simplistic and unrealistic. In the first section, "The Art of Being Human," we discussed differences in how people perceive things— the right versus the left side of the brain. The purpose of this chapter is to review and expand on that information as well as include information on learning preferences. In particular, this chapter asks, Is a person a visual, auditory, or kinesthetic learner, and does that student perceive better with the right or left half of the brain? In addition, the chapter discusses the concepts of experiential learning so that the field training officer will have a better understanding of the various differences in learning and gain insight on tailoring the class or training session more specifically to the needs of the trainee.

RIGHT-VERSUS LEFT-BRAIN LEARNING

To review, one concept of learning deals with the hemisphere, or area, of the brain that predominantly perceives and processes the information presented in a learning environment. While there is controversy as to the nature of the differences, let us recall that there are two hemispheres, or areas, of the brain—left and right, which perceive things uniquely. Fortunately, the two hemispheres or areas are connected, and the brain, as a whole, can process the material appropriately. However, if one area of the brain is significantly more dominant than the other, making sense of and processing new information can be challenging for the student.

These two areas of the brain look at the world differently. The left sees things analytically and verbally, while the right perceives things visually and perceptually. The following table breaks down the differences between the two.

Left	Right
Verbal—Uses words to describe	Nonverbal—Little connection with words
Analytic—Figures it out step-by-step	Synthetic—Puts things together to form a whole
Symbolic—Symbols represent things	Concrete—Relates to things in the present
Abstract—Small bit of information represents all	Analogic—Sees likenesses between things
Temporal—Keeps track of time	Nontemporal—No sense of time
Rational—Conclusions based on reason, fact	Nonrational—Not requiring basis of reason
Digital—Uses numbers, as in counting	Spatial—Sees things in relation to other things
Logical—Conclusion based on logic	Intuitive—Leaps of insight based on gut feelings
Linear—Thinks in linked ideas	Holistic—Sees whole things at once

In EMS education, we teach analytically, toward the left side of the brain. For example, we teach, "The signs and symptoms of a heart attack are a, b, c . . ." or "The treatment for shock is 1, 2, 3 . . ." This is a step-by-step, or analytical, approach to emergency care. However, the student who has learned the information with the left brain is placed into the "real world," where he or she has to process the scene from the right side of the brain. The student walks into a situation and finds a patient suffering from a heart attack. The patient does not say, "I am having a heart attack. List my signs and symptoms?" Rather, the patient is complaining of chest discomfort accompanied by the signs and symptoms of an acute myocardial infarction. Based on the scenario, the trainer is looking for the student to put it all together. The student, appearing baffled and bewildered, initially blunders through the scene.

Is it the student's fault? Perhaps, but we as instructors may have failed to recognize that the student might not be able to see the whole picture and process the scene from the right-brain perspective. The student is not necessarily a "slow learner" or incompetent to perform patient care. Rather, the student may be having trouble processing the information in the appropriate manner, seeing holistically rather than analytically.

To further illustrate this challenge, consider a rookie EMT accompanying a seasoned veteran on a call. The rookie, John, successfully completed the class, lab, and ride-along work required in any training program. Bill and John were dispatched to a "man down" call in a private residence. Arriving at the scene, John forgot to help Bill with the equipment and walked into the patient's apartment with a police officer. Bill got help from another officer and was able to get the jump kit and gurney into the residence.

Bill was shown into the small master bathroom, where he found John kneeling beside an unresponsive, older man. The patient was supine, snoring loudly, and did not respond to verbal or physical stimuli. First- and second-degree burns were evident on the man's left upper chest and upper left arm. Bill, the veteran EMT, standing five feet away, quickly sized up the situation and determined that the man had suffered a stroke while in the shower. As he fell, he either turned off the cold water or fully turned on the hot water, causing his burns. Seeing John at the man's side, Bill asked, "Whatcha got?" John replied, a bit panicky, "There's blood!" Bill responded, "Yes, and . . ." To which John plaintively reuttered, "There's blood."

What was the problem? John had been trained in the signs and symptoms of a stroke. He had been trained in recognizing second-degree burns. But John was not able to switch from the analytical mode into the holistic, see-the-whole-picture mode. In other words, John could not assimilate the scene and make an assessment of the man's problem. And, yes, John was a bit hyper.

The seasoned EMS professional has refined his holistic approach to a scene—seeing the whole picture immediately upon arriving. Think about the scene survey. Each time the ambulance arrives on the scene the EMT and paramedic size up the scene for hazards. How long does that process take? To the person adept at using the right brain, the scene survey is done before the ambulance comes to a stop. For the rookie who uses the left brain to analyze everything, it takes a lot longer.

In another example, consider the story about Frank and Jack getting lost during a call. After responding to a call in an unfamiliar area, Frank and Jack assessed, treated, and packaged the patient for transport to the emergency department. Frank was unsure of the routing to the hospital, so as he pulled away from the scene, he asked the dispatcher for directions. The dispatcher quickly gave the instructions: "Turn left onto Fourth Street, go to Ninth Avenue and turn right, then head to Fourteenth Street and . . ." After hearing the directions, Frank headed toward the hospital. In a few moments, though, he was hopelessly lost. He pulled to the side of the road, reached for the map book, and found his location and routing to the hospital—it was exactly as dispatch had said. What was the difference? Frank perceives things with the right brain. Hearing the direction in a logical, step-by-step fashion was foreign and incomprehensible. Reading the map put everything in perspective. He saw the whole picture—where he was and where he needed to go—and could navigate easily and safely.

An instructor will encounter these learning difficulties. Are there options that can be used to help the student overcome dominance in one area of the brain? Fortunately, there are a few things that can be used to stimulate developing the other side of the brain.

For the left-side-dominant person, have him or her draw pictures. Start out with simple illustrations, then draw more complex pictures over time. Drawing stimulates thoughts in the right side, or "whole picture," side of the brain. Another technique is to learn to read a map.

For the right-side dominant, have the student make lists of various things, particularly signs and symptoms or treatments for various conditions. In constructing lists of treatments, the list should be constructed in a sequential order. Also, have the student write directions traveling from one place to another. Finally, the student can also develop his or her math skills, especially when it comes to calculating drug doses. This will help the student begin to see things analytically.

I HEAR . . . I SEE . . . I DO

In addition to right- or left-brain processing, people have favored methods of learning. Most people have a primary style of learning, backed up by an ancillary learning style. One theory holds that these methods consist of visual, auditory, and kinesthetic or tactile learning styles. Another leading theory involves experiential learning developed by David Kolb and others.

VISUAL, AUDITORY, AND KINESTHETIC LEARNING STYLES

Visual, auditory, and kinesthetic learning styles refer to preferences in either seeing, hearing, or hands-on learning. People tend to have one preferred method, using a backup preference as necessary. To determine your preference between visual, auditory, and hands-on learning, complete the following self-assessment.

Learning Styles Assessment (Adapted from *Accelerated Learning*, by Colin Rose)

Read each statement and choose which best describes you most of the time:

1. When you spell a word, you:
   a. Try to see or picture the word.
   b. Sound out the word or use a phonetic approach.
   c. Write the word to see if it "feels" right.
2. When you talk with someone, you:
   a. Talk a little, but don't like listening for long periods of time.
   b. Enjoy listening, but are somewhat impatient waiting to talk.
   c. Gesture and use expressive movements when talking.
3. When you visualize or try to get a picture of something, you:
   a. See vivid, detailed pictures.
   b. Think with or in sounds.
   c. Have very few images, but the images involve movement.
4. When you are concentrating, you:
   a. Become distracted by movement or clutter or untidiness.
   b. Become distracted by sounds or noises like talking, radio, or television.
   c. Become distracted by activity around you.
5. When you meet someone, you:
   a. Forget names but remember faces or how you met the person.
   b. Forget faces but remember the names and the conversation.
   c. Remember what you and the other person did together.
6. When contacting people for business, you:
   a. Prefer a face-to-face personal meeting.
   b. Prefer calling the person on the phone.
   c. Prefer talking with them while walking or participating in an activity.
7. When you relax, you:
   a. Prefer watching television, movie, or a play.
   b. Prefer listening to the radio, stereo, or reading.
   c. Prefer to play games or do something with your hands.
8. When trying to interpret someone's mood, you:
   a. Look at facial expressions.
   b. Listen to the tone of the voice.
   c. Watch body movement or language.
9. When you are reading something, you:
   a. Prefer descriptive scenes when you can imagine the action.
   b. Enjoy the dialogue and conversation between characters.
   c. Like action stories or do not enjoy reading.
10. When doing something new at work, you:
    a. Like to see demonstrations, posters, diagrams, slides, or other teaching materials.
    b. Like verbal instructions or talking about the task with someone else.
    c. Just jump right in and try it, getting assistance as necessary.
11. When putting something together, you:
    a. Read the directions and look at the pictures.
    b. Talk out loud as you work or talk with someone else.
    c. Ignore the directions and figure things out as you go along.
12. When you need assistance with a computer program, you:
    a. Look for pictures or diagrams.
    b. Call technical support or the help desk.
    c. Keep trying to figure it out or try on another computer.

13. When you are teaching something to someone, you:
    a. Prefer showing the person the information.
    b. Prefer telling the person the information.
    c. Prefer letting the person see how it's done and then trying it.

Scoring:

Count the number of times you chose a, b, or c and total them below.

A. ________ Visual
B. ________ Auditory
C. ________ Kinesthetic (Tactile)

You will probably see responses in each area, with most responses falling in one area, several responses in a second style, and few responses falling in a third category. The area with the most answers indicates your primary learning style, whereas the category with the next highest number indicates your auxiliary learning style.

While you can assess a person's learning preference by giving them the above self-assessment, it might not be practical. In lieu of giving a written quiz, you might be able to detect differences in learning preferences by watching the students. The learning preferences might become evident in some of the behaviors listed below.

Visual Learner	Auditory Learner	Kinesthetic Learner
Uses facial expressions to express emotions	Uses different vocal tones and volume to express feelings	Physically expresses emotions
Enjoys examining things	Prefers someone reading to him than reading itself	Uses gestures when talking
Prefers to read	Prefers listening	Responds better to action words
Is more organized and quieter	May be heard mumbling when reading to self	Fidgets and cannot sit still
Quickly notices changes in classroom	Finds noises distracting	Has difficulty spelling and writes words to see if they feel right
Counts on fingers		

Visual Learning

Visual learners are those who process information by seeing things. Pictures, images, graphics, videotapes, and watching the instructor teach are ways that the visual learner processes the information. At times, a visual learner has to form a mental image of what and how someone is teaching in order to process the information better. The visual learner prefers looking at someone perform a skill before attempting that skill. They may not feel comfortable in a lab setting until they have had repeated opportunities to watch someone in action.

Where reading falls in preferred learning styles is controversial. Some would argue that reading is part of visual learning, while others, saying that we "hear" ourselves say the words, classify reading as auditory. Arguments can be made either way. To give an example of this confusion, consider the following sample e-mail, typed in all capital letters:

> MARY, I AM GIVING MY NEXT MAJOR EXAM ON PATIENT ASSESSMENT TOMORROW NIGHT AT 7 PM. PLEASE PRINT THIRTY

COPIES OF THE PATIENT ASSESSMENT TEST FOR MY CLASS TOMORROW. THANKS.

Did you have trouble with the note? According to e-mail "etiquette," typing in all capital letters looks like shouting. To others, the type style is inconsequential. Why do some people have trouble reading that text? A visual learner reads by looking at the shapes of the letters, not the individual letters. Since the shapes of the text are all capitals and large, the visual learner may have trouble differentiating the words and understanding the text.

Visual learners who are having difficulty with reading a text would benefit from watching videotapes or slides of the text. Most standard textbooks have accompanying slides or tapes that can be used to help the visual learner. More recently, some standard textbooks are using interactive learning on CD-ROM. Visual learners quickly adapt to the didactic information and case scenarios presented in this format.

Auditory Learning

Auditory learning consists of hearing the information. Students who favor this style need to hear the instructor, either in class or by audiotape. Those who prefer this method of learning pay close attention to the instructor and do well on quizzes or tests. Further, the auditory learners continue to do well outside of the classroom since they easily remember things said to them, making that information their own. People who have trouble hearing and remembering things should write notes for later reference. If reading is classified as auditory learning, rewriting or perhaps reciting the notes while reading them helps reinforce learning.

The auditory learner may seem to be a problem student when he or she is merely reiterating learned information. For example, the auditory learner may mutter something to him- or herself or to others nearby when the instructor is not speaking. It should be noted that these students are not intentionally disruptive, but are simply reinforcing auditory learning. If the mutterings are disruptive to the class, the instructor might gently remind the students to be a bit quieter.

Kinesthetic Learning

Kinesthetic learners want to sense position and movement. This type of learner, who is more tactile, wants to touch. Kinesthetic learners do extremely well in hands-on practical skill activities and prefer to "get their hands dirty." These students may not see the lecture as valuable, but will excel in a lab or practical setting. To help the kinesthetic learner who is having problems in the classroom, ask the student to apply the classroom learning, such as signs, symptoms, and treatment, in a practical setting. Incorporating both aspects of the training program for the kinesthetic learner will enhance the student's learning.

EXPERIENTIAL LEARNING STYLES

Another style of learning is a process known as experiential learning. In the early 1980s, Jack Mezirow and others suggested that the core to all learning was in the way we process an experience, especially how we look at or reflect upon that experience. During critical reflection, we analyze that experience and compare it with previous experiences to determine its impact.

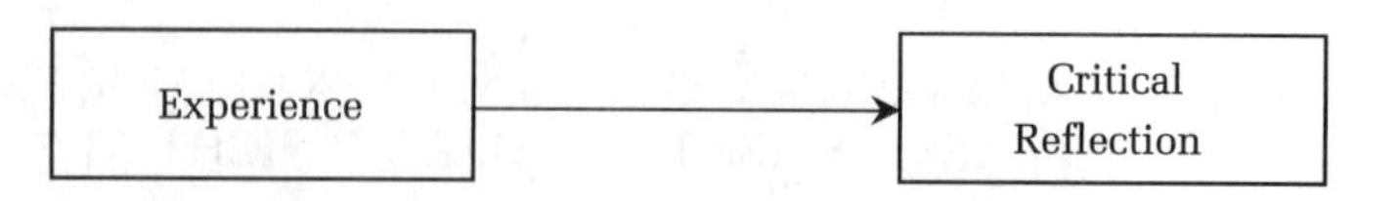

In the 1990s, David Kolb added two additional stages to the learning process—Abstract Conceptualization and Active Experimentation. With Abstract Conceptualization, a person seeks to understand the experience using logic and ideas instead of feelings. In Active Experimentation, a person actively engages in experimenting with or changing the situations into a form that works for the person. In essence, the person processes the experience into personalized learning, after which there is additional critical reflection. According to Kolb and others, this learning is cyclical.

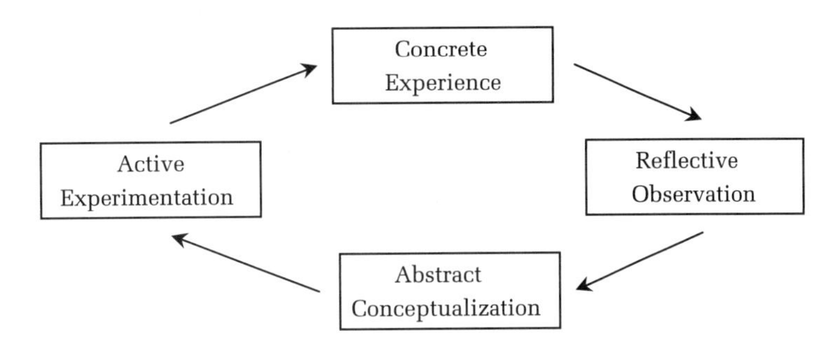

Kolb showed these learning styles as a continuum that a person will move through depending upon a learning situation. However, people tend to prefer one learning style to another and rely upon that style. For learners, these styles have specific preferences:

- *Concrete Experience:* Learner prefers being involved in a new experience, i.e., hands-on learning.
- *Reflective Observation:* Learner prefers brainstorming or active discussion to observe others.
- *Abstract Conceptualization:* Learner prefers lectures and analogies to develop theories as an explanation to what he or she has observed.
- *Active Experimentation:* Learner prefers simulations and case studies to solve problems and make decisions.

Before continuing, assess your experiential learning preferences with the following quiz. Circle the letter of the statement that best describes you:

A. I frequently come up with off-the-cuff ideas that initially might seem silly or strange.
B. I am thorough and methodical.
A. I am typically the person who starts conversations.
B. I am a people watcher.
A. I tend to be flexible and open-minded.
B. I tend to be careful and cautious.
A. I like to jump right in and try new or different things without much preparation.
B. I prefer to investigate something new like a topic or process in depth before trying it.
A. I am happy to try new things.
B. I draft lists of possible courses of actions before starting a new project.
A. I prefer to get involved and participate.
B. I prefer to read and observe.
A. I tend to be loud and outgoing.
B. I tend to be quiet and shy.

A. My decisions are quick and bold.
B. My decisions are made cautiously and logically.
A. I speak slowly after thinking.
B. I speak quickly, while thinking.
Total the number of A responses ________ and B responses ________.
If you have more As, you are dominant in the Active Experimentation style.
If you have more Bs, you are dominant in the Reflective Observation style.

Circle the letter of the statement that best describes you:

A. I probe for information when learning a new subject.
B. I pick up hints and techniques from other people.
A. I tend to be rational and logical.
B. I tend to be practical and down to earth.
A. I make detailed plans for events.
B. My plans are realistic, but flexible.
A. Before trying something new, I like to know the right answers.
B. I jump in and try things by practicing to see if they work.
A. I carefully analyze reports to find the basic assumptions and any inconsistencies.
B. I rely upon others to give me the nature of and basic information from reports.
A. I prefer working alone.
B. I enjoy working with other people.
A. Other people would consider me serious, reserved, and formal.
B. Other people would consider me verbal, expressive, and informal.
A. I make decisions based on facts.
B. I make decisions based on feelings.
A. I think that I am difficult to get to know.
B. I think that I am easy to get to know.
Total the number of A responses ________ and B responses ________.
If you have more As, you are dominant in Abstract Conceptualization.
If you have more Bs, you are dominant in Concrete Experience.

While Kolb's initial work suggested that these four styles of learning were cyclical, it became evident that there are actually two dimensions—grasping or perceiving the information and transforming or processing it.

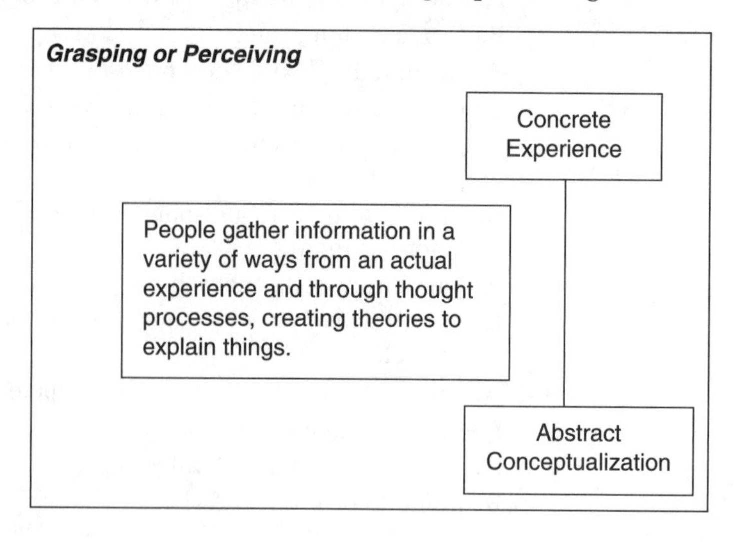

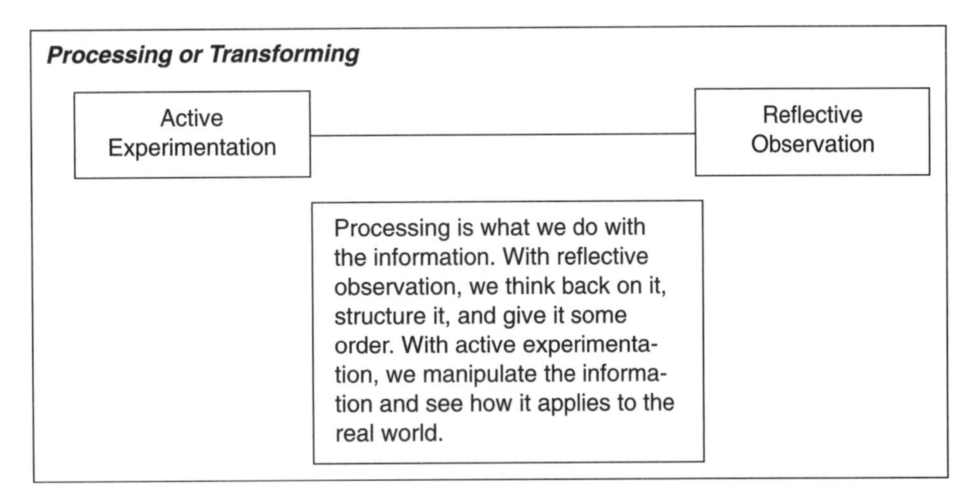

If we combine these two dimensions, we get four quadrants of learning styles.

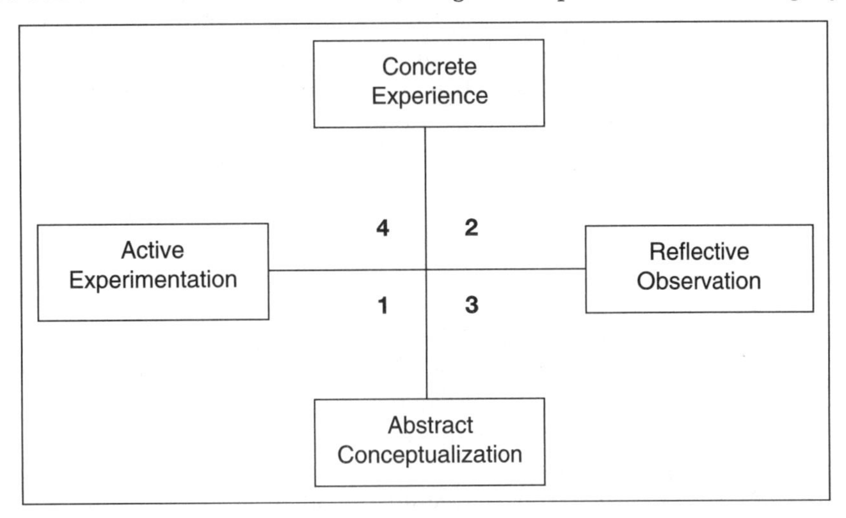

As you can see by the illustration, people tend to use two of these four learning styles to learn new information. Look back on the self-assessment above. Determine your two dominant learning styles and see where you fit in the above illustration. According to David Kolb and Donna Smith in *Learning Styles Inventory*, there will be differences in preferred learning depending upon which two styles are dominant. These four learning styles include:

Converger (1): Dominant learning styles are Abstract Conceptualization and Active Experimentation. These individuals excel in the practical application of ideas. Their knowledge is organized so that they can focus on problems using deductive reasoning. Convergers tend to be unemotional with narrow interests.

Diverger (2): Dominant learning styles are Concrete Experience and Reflective Observation. These individuals have a strong imagination and excel in the ability to look at situations from a variety of perspectives. They enjoy brainstorming and are interested in people.

Assimilator (3): Dominant learning styles include Abstract Conceptualization and Reflective Observation. These individuals excel at inductive reasoning and have a unique ability to take a variety of observations and develop a single, plausible explanation. Assimilators like the "facts" and want their theories to be logically sound.

Accomodator (4): Dominant learning styles include Concrete Experience and Active Experimentation. These individuals like doing things that involve new experiences. They take more risks and get more involved in trial-and-error problem solving. Accomodators tend to perform well when required to react to immediate circumstances.

HOW DO I KNOW WHAT TO USE?

The answer to this question is, you don't. However, the field training officer needs to be cognizant of learning difficulties and respond to the student who is having trouble. Investigating why that student is not learning will help the field training officer and employee formulate a better learning experience. For example, if an employee is an auditory learner and the training is predominantly lecture, allow the employee to tape the class to listen to the lecture later. The student can augment the tape by taking notes and rewriting them later. Different teaching techniques are discussed in Chapter 20.

The key to a successful class is to vary the method used in conducting the class. Frequently change from lecture to videotape to skill practice. Make the sessions different to appeal to the different learning preferences.

The instructor can influence visual learning through presentation. Of the following three things, which do you think best influences a student's learning? (See the section on "Being a Good Teacher.")

What you say.

What you look like (your appearance) while saying it.

How you say it.

If you picked the third one, you are right. Keeping a student's attention is very important in the learning process. While *what* you say might be extremely important information, if you are talking quietly or in a monotone, the student will tune you out and not listen. If, however, you vary the volume, pitch, and enthusiasm in your voice, the student will be more attentive and learn a lot more.

Your appearance is also important. However, you can be wearing an expensive suit while speaking on a valuable topic, but if you speak in a monotone, the student will probably learn very little.

For the learning styles identified by Kolb and Smith, the chart below may give you some insight on teaching techniques that can be incorporated into your presentations. In *Learning Styles Inventory*, Kolb and Smith identified teaching methods that can be used with various learning styles.

Converger	Diverger	Assimilator	Accomodator
• Self-paced exercises	• Small-group discussion	• Lecture	• Simulations
• Hands-on exploration	• Team exercises	• Independent reading/research	• Learning games
• Practical application of ideas	• Role-playing	• Detailed outline	• Active learning
• Case studies	• Brainstorming	• Data, facts, research	• Student presentations
• Individual projects	• Facilitator/learner coaching	• Case studies	• Applications to the real world
• Clear instructions	• Peer/tutor feedback	• Quizzes and tests	• Creating better ways

Another table of teaching methodologies for each learning style has been identified by Kathy Abbotsford (adapted from *Effective Teaching* using David Kolb's Theory on Learning Styles, http://instructordiploma.com/core/102B/abbotsford/kathy/htm)

Teaching Technique	Converger	Diverger	Assimilator	Accommodator
Lectures, demonstrations, Q and A	Lectures with examples	Lectures with chance to reflect	Short lectures	Lectures with slides
Demonstrations, group discussion, Q and A	Hands-on examples and demonstrations	Lectures with chance to reflect	Short lectures	Audiotape recordings
Brainstorming, role-playing	Feedback from peers	Brainstorming	Activities with problem solving	Feedback from peers
Projects	Activities to use skills	Short assignments with activities in class	Written papers	Case studies
Homework and projects	Opportunities to observe, workbooks	Group discussions, journals	Reading on theories, optional reading	Group discussions, extensive reading

As is evident, there are many ways to get the information across to the trainee. What works for some people will not work for others. Observing a trainee's difficulty and modifying it based on his or her preferences can enhance the trainee's grasp and understanding of the material.

SUMMARY

There are quite a few influences that determine a person's learning style. But, ultimately, learning has to be the choice of the student. A field training officer cannot force a student to learn anything he or she does not want to learn. However, if a trainee is having trouble grasping the information, perhaps changing the way it is delivered can make a difference. This chapter has presented information on learning styles and things that can influence learning. Right- and left-brain dominance can affect how information is perceived and processed. In addition, people tend to be visual, auditory, or kinesthetic learners, relying on specific senses more than others to gather information. Finally, people learn by experiencing things. That does not mean hands-on experience in all learning. Rather, it means that exposure to information leads to the experience that needs processing in order to be learned.

The field training officer can impact learning by recognizing different learning styles and modifying the presentation of information based upon the preferences of the trainee. By changing the presentation technique, the field training officer can get the information to the employee in a way that the employee enjoys the experience and learns.

14

Teaching the Adult

Most EMS instructors have a lot of field experience, but how many have formal training in classroom instruction, especially in teaching adults? The purpose of this chapter is to take a look at some important concepts of adult learning and illustrate how they can apply to the EMT and paramedic student in the classroom.

ADULTS ARE NOT THE SAME AS CHILDREN

As previously mentioned, the approach to the adult learner in the classroom is considerably different from the approach that our fourth-grade teacher used when we were in grade school. These differences are important since the adult learner comes to class with a different attitude toward learning. In his book *Modern Practice,* first published in 1970, Malcolm Knowles popularized the term *andragogy* to reflect the teaching of adults. Over the years, various authors have argued the points that Knowles discussed. Yet there are four basic assumptions of andragogy that have persisted through the years.

Adults want control of and responsibility for their learning.

Adults bring various life experiences to the classroom.

Adult learning is often problem centered—learning to solve a life problem.

Adults are motivated to learn from within—intrinsic motivation.

Knowing these assumptions on adult learning, EMS educators can look upon the teaching experience not as an instructor, but as a facilitator of learning. Based upon this general premise of teaching, the EMS educator can modify the classroom experience to best suit the needs of adult students.

IN THE CLASSROOM

In 1984, Ronald and Susan Zemke published "30 Things We Know for Sure About Adult Learning" (*Innovation Abstracts,* vol. 6, no. 8). There is a wealth of information contained in thirty brief comments. Of particular note are the Zemkes' thoughts on the adult learner in the classroom. Perhaps we in EMS education can take note of some of their observations:

"The learning environment must be physically and psychologically comfortable; long lectures, periods of interminable sitting, and the absence of practice opportunities rate high on the irritation scale." This observation is especially

keen for initial EMT and paramedic training. Think about one of the basic tenets of education that were mentioned earlier in the section, especially. . .

The brain can absorb as long as the butt can endure.

The adult has a body that is strongly influenced by gravity. Sitting for long periods of time can be unbearable. A ninety-minute session is about the longest many adults can sit without becoming uncomfortable, especially at the typical classroom desk.

An interesting comment about the above observation is the concept of the classroom being "psychologically comfortable." Sitting at a desk offers more than a place to write. It also offers some form of barrier between the teacher and student as well as between students. This barrier often allows the student to communicate more freely with the facilitator and the class. Not having a desk or table in front of the student can invite the student to feel defensive. Consider the differences in atmosphere when the students are seated at a desk (or table) as opposed to sitting in a plain chair, especially if the chairs are formed in a circle.

"Adults have something real to lose in a classroom situation. Self-esteem and ego are on the line when they are asked to risk trying a new behavior in front of peers and cohorts." Adults have pride. Pride is a concept that is downplayed as if it is not an important trait. But it is still present. Imagine being asked to perform a skill in front of peers and failing. Adults will not ask questions or participate in a practical skills demonstration if they are afraid of being discounted or put down for an error, especially if the instructor corrects the skill or embarrasses the student in front of the class. Allow the student to admit that he or she does not know the answer to a question or how to perform a skill.

When asking a student to demonstrate a new skill, be sure the student has been given the opportunity to practice it beforehand. Also, give the student an "out"—permission to decline the request to demonstrate the skill. Finally, rather than selecting a student at random, ask for volunteers. Some students are more comfortable than others when demonstrating something new.

After a student answers a question or performs the skill, thank the student. Treating the student with respect will go a long way to helping the student learn.

"Adults have expectations, and it is critical to take time early on to clarify and articulate all expectations before getting into content." Depending on the nature of the training session, it might be beneficial to ask the participants what they expect to get out of the training session. The student's expectations may be different from those of the instructor. If so, the objectives of the program should be reiterated and modified if necessary. In advertised training sessions, the nature and scope of the course is usually clearly spelled out. Often, students do not read this information and come to a class looking for something different, yet similar to what is being offered.

"Adults bring a great deal of life experience into the classroom, an invaluable asset to be acknowledged, tapped, and used." Some EMT and paramedic students have a tremendous background in medical-related fields. Some may have served in a medical capacity in the military, while others may have worked in a hospital or physician's office. This experience is important and can be used to enhance the classroom experience of the other students. Since all new information has to be integrated with previous knowledge, past experiences can also be used to help the student more easily incorporate the new information.

Of course, poor or inappropriate life experiences need to be corrected. One student, after experiencing his first ride-along, discussed his experience with the class. Based on his presentation of the ride-along, certain techniques were not up to "standard." At the beginning of his discussion, the student proudly boasted, "I have seen reality." Unfortunately, the reality he experienced was not very good. A private counseling session to correct the perception was appropriate.

"The key to the instructor role is control. The instructor must balance the presentation of new material, debate and discussion, sharing of relevant student experiences, and the clock. Ironically, it seems that instructors are best able to establish control when they risk giving it up. When they shelve egos and stifle the tendency to be threatened by challenges to plans and methods, they gain the kind of facilitative control needed to effect adult learning." In pedagogical teaching, the instructor is seen as lord and commander of the classroom. The students depend totally on the teacher for the classroom and learning experience. Adult learners are different. As mentioned earlier, the adult's life experiences play a key role in his or her learning. Allowing time to share those experiences with the rest of the class may throw the schedule off track. So what. Being flexible and adaptive in the classroom actually gives the instructor more control over the activities.

Further, EMS instructors need to remember that there is more than one way of doing most things. There will be times when a student shares a technique that the instructor has never seen. Does it mean that the skill is wrong? No. Adults learn best when sharing information among peers. Keep in mind, the instructor is also a peer. Wayne Dyer once said, "This is my way. What is your way? The way does not exist." Not only do the students learn from the instructor, the instructor can learn from the students.

Traditional education as you have probably experienced it in grammar, grade, middle, and high school is based upon the educational theory known as pedagogy. *Pedagogy* is from the Greek word meaning "leading of children." This theory makes certain assumptions which might not be sound when teaching adults.

Andragogy, the term made popular by Professor Malcom Knowles, means "helping adults learn" and is commonly referred to as adult learning, adult education, or life-long learning. This technique of education incorporates aspects of teaching that tremendously assist learning. Such aspects include professionalism, self-assurance, understanding, compassion, and responsibility.

In adult education, the basic belief is that the student is a "complete" person capable of making rational decisions about the information he or she chooses to learn. It also believes that the student has chosen to be in the learning program. You might say the field training program is required for the employee; therefore, the adult *must* attend. While that is true, the adult can choose to leave his or her employment and work elsewhere. Below are the differences between the philosophies of pedagogy and andragogy.

Pedagogy	Andragogy
Sees education as the constant preparation for the future	Sees education as relevant to the present as well as to the future
Assumes the attitude of compulsory attendance regardless of the student's interest in the subject matter	Recognizes that the student will attend class only as long as he or she is gaining valuable knowledge and not wasting time
Assumes the student is dependent and in need of direction by someone possessing superior knowledge	Recognizes that the student is independent and capable of self-direction, but for this subject is asking for guidance in learning

Views the teacher as having superior knowledge in all aspects of the subject	Recognizes that the teacher is also human and that education is a reciprocal relationship
Views the teacher's experience and knowledge as primary sources for learning	Sees the student's experience as well as the instructor's as valuable learning resources
Insists the teacher decide what will be learned, how it will be taught, and under what conditions learning will take place	Invites the student to take an active role in areas of special interest for what will be learned and under what conditions
Assumes that how well something is learned outweighs the student's feelings about what is learned	Assumes that the student's feelings about the subject greatly influence the retention of material, learning quality increases
Believes that the student's life experiences are essentially superfluous	Believes the student's life experiences are vital to the learning process
Regards the student as incapable of deciding the value of the learning or need for further learning	Regards the student as capable of deciding the value of the education and need for further learning

MOTIVATING THE ADULT LEARNER

In the first section, "The Art of Being Human," we discussed some of the factors that motivate people, such as meeting basic needs, obtaining strokes, and similar drivers. While we can use this information to help motivate the trainees to learn, we need to consider other factors that motivate adults to learn.

To understand some techniques that will motivate the trainee, it is important to understand some additional concepts relevant to the adult learner. First, adults are autonomous and self-directed. In other words, they need to be free to direct their own learning. As an instructor, you cannot force learning, but merely invite it.

Adults have life experiences that play a key role in their attitude toward learning new information. Use the trainee's past experiences to draw out information that is relevant to the topic. An adult who feels he or she has contributed to the class will feel better about learning new information.

Keep in mind that adults want information that is useful to their lives or work. Something that will never be used or has no relevance will be resisted.

So, what motivates the adult to learn? Stephen Lieb, Instructor at South Mountain Community College in Arizona, identified six factors that motivate an adult to learn. These include:

- Social relationships—Making new friends or new associations
- External expectations—Complying with instructions to attend the program
- Social welfare—Preparing for service to a community or to perform community work
- Personal advancement—Seeking promotion at work or keeping up with current trends
- Escape or stimulation—Relieving boredom or get away from the routine of life
- Cognitive interest—Learning just to learn

While some of the above factors will play a role in student motivation, some obviously are not relevant. However, you can use some of these factors when considering how to motivate the student or trainee to learn.

First, consider the learning environment. If you are using a classroom to teach, make sure that the classroom has a warm and accepting environment. It should also be businesslike. This type of atmosphere will promote positive attitudes toward learning. When possible and permissible, place visual aids such as charts, graphs, or practice equipment in the room. These training aids capture the attention and curiosity of the student.

Use external rewards judiciously. Look back to Section 1 and review the Locus of Control quiz. Internal or intrinsic rewards tend to last longer than external rewards. While external rewards are important for status and esteem, such rewards must be continuous and concrete in nature. Use caution and prudence when giving external rewards since excessive use could cause a decrease in internal motivation.

As a field training officer, you can encourage learning, but a trainee will only learn when he or she is ready. A student who is not ready to learn may have to be repeatedly told what and how to do something, which can be frustrating for both the student and instructor.

Organize your materials. A student is more apt to learn when the information is organized and makes sense, especially if the information is linked to something the student already does. This also pertains to teaching information that the trainee, as an adult, finds valuable. If the adult learner feels the information is irrelevant and has no value to him or her personally or professionally, learning will be avoided. When possible, tie in the material to something that the trainee feels is important. For example, if you are teaching a skill that will never be used in the field, do not expect the trainee to be enthusiastic about the experience or even learn the new skill.

Make sure the student has goals that are realistic and achievable. If a student set unrealistic goals that cannot be achieved, repeated failure will decrease motivation and could lead to the student's losing interest in the class.

Learning something new requires a change in beliefs and behavior that can cause anxiety in the student. As such, a trainee will be under stress in any learning situation. Your responsibility is to recognize excessive stress and help alleviate it so that the trainee can learn the information. As an instructor, you have the responsibility to avoid causing too much stress or anxiety in your students by setting overly aggressive or ambiguous goals.

Finally, give quick feedback. If you will be teaching a class that includes written tests or practical examinations, let the students know what is expected of them. For written quizzes or tests, be clear what will be covered on the exam. For skills, give the student a copy of the skills checklist so that he or she knows the level of performance to be achieved. However, deemphasize grades. The weight of a grade can be a positive or negative motivator. A C student may know as much as an A student, yet the C student might have problems with written tests. Emphasize learning and proficiency instead of a percentage of right answers.

After an exam, provide prompt feedback. If you grade an exam immediately after the student completes it, give the student his or her score at that time. Do not wait until the end of the class to give feedback on a test. Be sure to reward a student's successes, even if the overall performance might be less than satisfactory. Letting the trainee know that you think he or she will improve over time can be a strong motivator to keep trying.

Other Thoughts on Motivating the Adult Learner

Motivating the adult learner is similar to motivating the employee. Many of the management principles found in the *One-Minute Manager* can be applied to the teaching situation:

Praise the student immediately. If a student is taking a written examination, give him or her the results as soon as possible. Waiting for the results can be nerve-wracking. Also, if a student has done exceptionally well, offer praise in front of other students. If you are grading a written examination, give points instead of taking them away. For example, if John Doe missed 10 out of 100 questions, write +ninety on his paper rather than −10. You can also draw a "smiley face" on the paper showing that you are pleased with the work. Emphasizing the positive motivates students more than emphasizing the negative.

Tell the student what he or she did right and be specific. If a particular skill has been evaluated and the student did exceptionally well, let the student know. People enjoy being complimented in front of their peers.

Pause for a moment to let the student feel how good you feel. You can be proud of the student and of your accomplishment. It is because of your guidance that the student succeeded.

Offer encouragement to keep up the good work. Tell the student you are proud of his or her accomplishments.

Unfortunately, there will be times when criticism is necessary. Like one-minute praising, there is a one-minute criticism, which works best when you:

Tell the student up-front that you are going to let them know how they are doing. Let the student immediately know the nature of the conversation. It can be upsetting to have a conversation end with "Oh, by the way, we need to talk about your performance."

Deliver a critique immediately, but out of earshot of other students. It would be preferable to critique a student in a closed office or room. Do not announce to the world that you are taking a student into a closed-door session. He or she will be sufficiently embarrassed just by having the meeting.

Tell the student what he or she did wrong and be specific. In order to improve, a person needs to know the details of their weaknesses.

Reaffirm that you think well of them but not their performance. No one likes to be discounted or made to feel badly about themselves.

Recognize that when a critique is over, it is over. Students resent reminders. Dwelling on a problem can be humiliating. Move on to something else after the critique.

There are other techniques to use in motivating the adult learner. These include:

- Developing and reinforcing a positive self-image in the student.
- Telling students that success is possible if they, at least, try.
- Making learning fun.
- Setting and communicating high expectations. Let the students strive to come up to the instructor's level of expectations.
- Having confidence in the self and displaying that self-confidence to the students.
- Emphasizing knowledge and skill performance, not grades.
- Not playing favorites—treating everyone the same.
- Making the class interactive or using media that stimulates interaction with students.
- Alleviating test anxiety.
- Presenting the material in a dynamic way to make students want to come to class.

SUMMARY

This chapter has focused on teaching the adult. Unlike teaching children, adults bring to the training session their life's experiences and rely upon those to aid in the learning process. Adults want to get something from the session that will be beneficial to them either professionally or personally. The field training officer needs to be aware of the differences between and adults and children in a teaching environment so that he or she can obtain the trainee's acceptance and stimulate learning in the workplace.

15

The Students You'll See

Behavioral Issues in the Classroom

Adult learners come in all shapes, sizes, and types. In teaching adults, it is important to know about the types of students you will see in your classes, since it will affect how you will conduct your class or training session. While it would be nice if all of our students were academically inclined and enthusiastic learners, there are some trainees who can be a challenge to even the most veteran instructor. This chapter will familiarize you with the different types of students and offer suggestions on how to handle problem behaviors in a classroom or other setting.

As a field training officer who conducts one-on-one or small-group training, you will meet each of the various types of students. Some of these are more commonly encountered in initial or continuing education programs; however, field trainers may also see any number of student types. The types of participants include the Vacationer, Prisoner, Adventurer, VIP, Worrier, and Challenger. Each poses challenges to classroom management, since they may or may not want to participate in the learning session.

Vacationer. As the name implies, this trainee or student is in a vacation mode—no calls or routine tasks, only time to relax. The Vacationer is not in any hurry to finish assignments and occasionally will not complete some tasks unless there is a pressing reason to finish them. If the Vacationer is in a classroom setting, he or she may take long lunches or breaks. He or she may even mention

coming to class late or leaving early. After all, this person is on vacation from the rigors of the job and sometimes away from the demands of the family. If the Vacationer arrives late or leaves early, do not attempt to bring him or her "up to speed." Rather, you might need to remind the Vacationer of the responsibilities in the training program, including the importance of being on time.

Prisoner. The Prisoner is a tough one to handle. This student or trainee is resistant to anything and everything you want to present. He or she will display closed body language such as crossed arms or pursed lips, and acts as if there is no time for this "nonsense." He or she feels as if they are "serving time" for some unknown grievance. Often, the Prisoner is in class because of a job requirement. When giving handouts, the Prisoner may roll the eyes and mutter something like "Just what I need, more crap." The Prisoner frequently looks at the clock and asks or hints at breaks from class. A common question the Prisoner asks is "When is the class going to be over?" Getting this type of student to participate can be difficult. You might need to treat him or her like the heckler on the scene of a call—by getting the person involved, making the person feel that he or she is contributing to the class, and that others benefit from that participation.

Adventurer. The Adventurer is the type of person who seems to enjoy life and looks at life and learning as an adventure. This type of student will usually sit

at the front of the class, often arriving early and staying late to ask questions—a lot of questions. At times, the Adventurer might become a bit obnoxious. You might need to counsel the student during a break or after class, asking him or her to ask less questions or allow others to ask them.

VIP. This student perceives him- or herself as a "Very Important Person" and tends to have a negative attitude toward training. The VIP lets you know that he or she is doing you a favor by attending the class. According to the VIP, he or she already knows all the information that will be presented and knew it even before the instructor. Because this student already knows everything, he or she does not pay attention and misses directions and assignments. The cell phone will also be conspicuously on the desk and, if it rings, the VIP must answer it, even during class. Because of their VIP status, he or she will frequently need to leave the classroom to use the phone. This type of student may look for power and phone outlets to connect a laptop computer while spreading out an appointment book. If you do not acknowledge the VIP, he or she may pout. To overcome a negative attitude, you can call on the VIP's knowledge and experience to help with the class and assist in "teaching" the material. The VIP might best help in discussing how to apply the information in real-life situations. To avoid missing assignments, you might need to remind the VIP or have him or her restate the assignment or directions to the class.

Worrier. This student is in a near-panic state; worried that he or she will not pass the test, skill, or, even worse, the course. He or she sits near the front of the class either recording the lecture or trying to write down everything that is said, often asking to repeat or clarify something that was just covered. He or she may hang around after class or arrive early, hoping to get more information or be reassured about passing. Often, these students will have high marks on exams but fear they are near failing, especially if their grade is less than an A. Low self-image could contribute to the distressed nature of this student. Reassurances will be calming—for a while. Occasionally, you may have to give this type of student positive feedback to allay fears.

Challenger. This student, similar to the VIP, loves a challenge and may believe that he or she already has the knowledge or information. Frequently, the Challenger will find something different in the book than what you discussed in class and bring it up in front of the rest of the students. This seems more like a mind game and an attempt to undermine the instructor. Your response to the Challenger will depend on a few factors. First, if time permits and you feel comfortable; you can answer the challenge in class. Otherwise, tell the student that you will be happy to discuss his or her concerns during a break or after class. If

the Challenger is right, acknowledge it. If he or she is partly correct, also acknowledge it, but give the correct and complete information. If the Challenger is incorrect, this also needs to be addressed. Should the problem worsen and the Challenger become disruptive, a private counseling session might be in order.

In addition to the types of students you will encounter in your classroom or training session, you may see problem behaviors that could create a classroom management dilemma. The problem behaviors include Broken Record, Dominator, Interrupter, Dropout, and Chatterbox.

Broken Record tends to repeat the same point and attempts to focus the group on a single issue, usually one that only he or she is concerned about. Broken Record prevents the class from progressing and can be frustrating not only to the instructor, but also the entire class. To combat Broken Record, reassure him or her that you heard the point and, if necessary, document it on a chalkboard or easel and pad to address later in the session. If Broken Record repeats the point, refer to the chalkboard and say that the topic will be discussed when time permits or the direction has turned to that particular topic.

Dominator is a participant who talks too much and too often. Occasionally, it becomes difficult to quiet Dominator. Should this behavior interfere with the class, stand next to him or her for a few minutes to divert the conversation. Once Dominator feels your presence, the conversation will stop. Then, thank Dominator for the contribution to the class while asking for other participants' ideas or thoughts. If the behavior continues, a counseling session during a break would be appropriate.

Interrupter tends to cut people off, perhaps being concerned that his or her thoughts may not be heard or addressed adequately. To combat this behavior, politely stop Interrupter, allowing the person who was speaking to continue. After the other person has finished, return to Interrupter and allow him or her to continue. Do not allow Interrupter to continuously interrupt others.

Dropout tends to sit alone in the back of the room, away from the desk or table. Like the Prisoner, he or she disapproves of the session and displays disapproval by ignoring the instructor. Dropout may doodle or do other work during the class. To get Dropout's attention, look directly and intensely at him or her for a few moments. This lets Dropout know that you are aware of the behavior and do not approve. To bring the person into the group, ask Dropout a question or two pertaining to his or her experiences with the topic being presented. If Dropout refuses to participate, do not force the issue, but speak to him or her during a break.

Chatterbox is always talking, usually whispering to a classmate during the presentation. Unlike Dominator, who may be talking about the topic, Chatterbox may be discussing anything, including personal information. Handling Chatterbox is similar to responding to Dominator. Position yourself next to Chatterbox and, when the conversation ends, remind the entire class that it would be best to only have one person speaking at a time. Persistent talking after the interruption can be handled by asking the person if he or she has something to add to the class discussion.

The student types and problem behaviors above can be trying, especially when the topic and time constraints precluding spending a lot of time on classroom management. By understanding the cause and nature of the problem behavior, you can gain control of the class early and make the training session more enjoyable for everyone, including you.

SUMMARY

This chapter has taken a look at the various types of learners you as a field training officer will see in a classroom or other instruction environment. Each one of these types of trainees poses unique challenges that can test your abilities as an EMS instructor.

16

Making Your Point!

Teaching Metholodologies for the EMS Instructor

While a good teacher has many qualities, one of those qualities is the ability to determine the teaching method that will work best for a group of students or a program of instruction. There are several teaching methodologies that the EMS educator can use, depending on the class being taught. These methodologies include lecture or lecture/discussion, brainstorming, video- and audiotapes, case studies, role-playing, flash cards, and use of a guest speaker. The purpose of this chapter is to briefly discuss each teaching method and present its strengths and weaknesses, allowing the EMS instructor to decide which method would be best to meet specific needs.

Lecture

A commonly used methodology is the lecture. A lecture method is being used when the instructor presents information by speaking to an audience, such as at a seminar or conference where a large number of people are attending. There is no interaction between the speaker and the group. The strength of the lecture method includes the presentation of factual material in an orderly and logical manner. It can stimulate thinking for later discussion and is a good method for presenting information to large groups of participants.

The lecture method also has drawbacks. If a subject matter expert presents the information, he or she may not be a good instructor or speaker. Occasionally, subject matter experts delve so deeply into the material that the audience loses interest. Another drawback to the lecture method is that learning is one-way. There is no provision for audience feedback, and it is difficult to gauge how much learning has occurred.

Lecture/Discussion

In a lecture/discussion, some lecture-only weaknesses are overcome. Using this method, after the material has been presented, there is interaction between the teacher and the students. Depending on time constraints, it may be easier to determine how much, if any, learning has occurred by the nature of the questions. If the students do not have any questions when the discussion begins, the instructor can have prepared questions (frequently asked questions—FAQs) that can be used to get the question-and-answer session started.

Discussion

Discussion can be used alone as a teaching method, since it makes use of ideas and experiences from the entire group. It invites active participation from all students. However, a discussion should be limited to groups of less than twenty people, otherwise the discussion can become unfocused. Also, a discussion can allow one person to dominate, inviting others in the group to feel intimidated. The instructor needs to balance active participation by students to avoid one person taking control of the group activity.

Brainstorming

Brainstorming is an intense listening exercise that stimulates creative thinking for problem solving or developing new ideas. Each participant in the group is invited to share equally, since all ideas are recorded on a chalkboard or easel and pad. The easel and pad pages can be taped to the wall for continued reference. Brainstorming will make use of each person's knowledge and experience, allowing ideas to generate or spark off other ideas. This can be ideal in a one-on-one situation where the instructor needs to elicit the trainee's information and spark his or her imagination. It can be done easily after a call to critique or analyze the trainee's performance. Brainstorming can also be conducted in a classroom after didactic instruction has given the students a base of information. For example, with a small group of students, the instructor can pose a hypothetical case study (also see case studies below). Basic information such as age, weight, and chief complaint are given. The group is then instructed to ask questions as if examining a patient. The instructor gives diagnostic information as it is requested. The group brainstorms the assessment and treatment for the hypothetical case.

There are several drawbacks to brainstorming. First, a large group can get out of control and lose focus quickly. To reduce the possibility for loss of control, limit brainstorming to less than ten minutes. Another problem with group brainstorming is that it can lead to criticizing and evaluating one or more of the participants. Any negative comments toward a member of the group could cause the affected student to withdraw from future activities.

Video- and Audiotapes

Using video- and audiotapes can be a fun and entertaining way of teaching a part of the program. High-quality tapes look professional, keep the participants' attention, and stimulate discussion. Videotapes can also be used to assess skill performance. If role-play is used, videotaping the scene can invite the "rescuers" to critique themselves. An instructor will often find that students are more critical of themselves than the instructor would be.

A drawback to video- or audiotape presentations is that they may only stimulate minimal participation during the discussion afterward. Because of the nature of video- and audiotapes, a number of important issues can be presented, and any follow-up discussion can become unfocused or disjointed. It is important for the instructor to have a list of discussion questions to be raised after using the tape. When reviewing a videotaped scene, the instructor can begin the critique and let the students proceed. The instructor should always find some good points to highlight and not focus on the negative. For example, for every negative comment, the instructor should provide feedback on at least three positive aspects of the scenario. This same rule also applies if the scenario was chaotic and not well performed.

Case Studies

Using case studies is an excellent way to highlight important points. This invites the students to use analytical problem-solving skills and explore real-life situations in a question-and-answer format. By incorporating case studies, the student can make use of and reinforce new information.

A drawback to using a case study is the preparation time. The instructor must carefully plan the case study, including the diagnostic signs and clinical findings if using patient scenarios. One case study method that has been used successfully consists of presenting a general overview of the situation and then having each student ask one question, getting information as he or she would in the field.

An example of case study is as follows. You are called to a private residence, where you are greeted by a frantic woman telling you that her six-year-old son is unconscious. She hurriedly leads you into the house and child's bedroom, where you find the child in a supine position on the bed.

Example of questions the group might ask are: What are his vital signs? What is his skin temperature?

Role-Playing

Another technique used quite successfully in EMS education is the role-play. This teaching method dramatically introduces problem solving in a lower-stress situation. A patient case scenario is developed using manikins or other students, and the trainee is asked to assess the scene or perform certain skills during the scene. This technique allows the student to practice and hone skills. An adjunct to the role-play is videotaping the scenario, as discussed earlier.

In some educational environments, some students may feel threatened or self-conscious. In EMS education, nearly all students have to participate in role-playing; thus, the student's apprehension tends to be lessened. Role-plays do require that the instructor clearly define the situation and what is to be expected of each participant. In most cases, a check sheet is provided as a tool for scoring the trainee's performance and evaluating progress. In addition to clearly defining the role of the student, the instructor must carefully determine the role of the "patient" to include chief complaint, diagnostic signs, and other pertinent information. Once the scenario has been designed, the instructor must inform the "patient" of his or her condition as well as the signs and symptoms.

Flash Card

Preparing index cards is a great tool for self-study or learning in small groups. Index cards are difficult to use in a large group because of the nature of the technique. On one side of an index card, the instructor writes a question. The reverse side of the card contains the answer. Using flash cards reinforces learning, especially the memorization of new information. Used later, flash cards are an effective tool to reinforce knowledge. A variation on this same theme is a "Jeopardy"-like game that has categories and values for each question in a category. Teams can be created to compete against each other.

A drawback to using flash cards is that many trainees will not do the exercise or may stop the exercise early in the study session because of lack of interest or distractions inside or out of the classroom. Another drawback is that the instructor must prepare the cards well in advance if the cards will be used in class.

SOME TIPS ON *GOOD* TEACHING

Effective instruction depends on many components, which include an appropriate teaching method and style for the situation, as well as a lesson plan for the subject to be presented. It also depends on other factors that are less concrete. These more abstract ideas make up what might be called good teaching. Thus, the purpose of this section is twofold. First, it will highlight some factors of being a good teacher based upon thoughts published by a professor at a major university. Second, this section will give you food for thought. In reading this infomation, think about the aspects of being a good teacher that you can use to enhance your abilities and make teaching a lot more fun.

An article by Richard Leblanc of York University appeared in 1998 in *The Teaching Professor.* It was entitled "Good Teaching: The Top Ten Requirements" and listed ten fundamentals of being a good teacher. Several of these requirements are presented and discussed here to help you become a better teacher.

Good Teaching. . .

"Is as much about passion as it is about reason." A good instructor will motivate students in ways that are relevant and meaningful. The EMS instructor must be passionate about teaching and must share that passion with students and colleagues. Sure, there will be days when your enthusiasm will be dampened. But those days pass quickly. If teaching becomes a drag and the downside does not let up, it might be time to take a break and "recharge your batteries."

"Is about substance and treating students as consumers of knowledge." As a teacher, the EMS instructor must keep up-to-date with current trends in prehospital care. Subscribing to trade journals, searching the Internet, making outside contacts, consulting with experts, and developing a voracious appetite for learning new and relevant information is critical to the EMS educator's success. People enjoy learning. Adults are hungy for information that is relevant to their jobs or that they can use in their personal lives. A good teacher recognizes that the participant in a class is not only a student, but a customer as well—a consumer of the information being presented. As such, the instructor provides a much-needed service to the consumers of knowledge. If the customer feels that there is no value in the class, he or she will not stay in the class for long.

"Is about listening, questioning, being responsive, and remembering that each student and each class is different." Do not be afraid to ask, Why? Even more important, do not be afraid to ask, Why not? The students you see over the years will be asking these questions—sometimes in a challenging way. Over the years we have seen many changes in prehospital care. Often, a piece of equipment or technique is touted as lifesaving, only to be challenged, studied, and ultimately changed or discarded. For those who have been in EMS over the past few decades, think about the MAST device or stair-step ventilation in CPR. Also, remembering that each class is different helps keep things in perspective. When you find yourself thinking, "If I have to give this lecture one more time, I am going to . . ." It might be the umpty-umpth time you have given the lecture or seen the slides, but it is likely the students' first time seeing or hearing the information.

"Is about being flexible and fluid, experimenting, and having the confidence to react and respond to changing circumstances." There will be challenging days when only a small portion of the scheduled training program is presented. The reasons for altering the program can be numerous, but be flexible and adaptive enough to go with the flow. Make changes as necessary for the benefit of the student or the class.

"Is about style. Should good teaching be entertaining? You bet!" A good teacher will "work the room" and be informative as well as entertaining. Avoid droning or speaking in a monotone while staring at the back wall or projection screen. Be animated and enthusiastic. Three things that can make a difference in your students' learning—what you say, what you look like when saying it, and how you say it—but how you present the material can make a huge difference in the level of learning in the group.

"Is about humor." The use of innocuous jokes and self-deprecating humor brings the teacher down to a more human level. It has been shown that, when used appropriately, humor can increase students' learning. They will enjoy the class and pay more attention to the information being presented.

"Is about caring, nurturing, and developing minds and talents." Spend extra time with a student whenever needed. If you see that a student is having trouble, ask if he or she needs help. Sometimes the student is afraid of asking since it might be a sign of not being "smart enough." Some students will ask for help. They may want additional homework or directions on how to get more information on a topic. Take the time to nurture all students. Even though that extra time may be invisible to other students or your supervisor, it will mean a lot to the student receiving the extra assistance. In addition, the student's success will give you intrinsic rewards that cannot be matched by anything else.

"Is about having fun, experiencing pleasure, and receiving intrinsic rewards." When teaching, have fun. Enjoy the class, be relaxed, and use the time to feel good about what you are doing. Laugh, smile, and fully enjoy the interaction with the students. When you are having fun in the class, your enjoyment is transferred to the students and they begin to look forward to coming to class. As they become more involved in the training, you will notice something like a "light" coming on when a student "gets" the material. This is an intrinsic reward—something that no one can giftwrap and hand out. It makes you smile on the inside. Getting that intrinsic reward and having fun while teaching will keep you coming back to the classroom.

SUMMARY

A good teacher has many qualities, one of which includes the ability to present information in an effective way. But good teaching means a lot more that presenting information. Incorporating these attributes will enhance your experiences as an EMS educator. This chapter presents information on teaching techniques as well as discussion of concepts that will help make you, the field training officer, an excellent instructor.

17

Tools of the Trade

Every occupation has its own tools and techniques of the trade. EMTs and paramedics use emergency medical equipment to provide quality patient care. Similarly, the EMS instructor will have tools that can help the trainee learn better. This chapter will briefly describe the tools that the field training officer may use and give you some tips to avoid last-minute disasters.

AUDIOVISUAL AIDS

Most classrooms are equipped with audiovisual aids such as a chalkboard or dry erase board, slide and overhead projectors, slides and overhead transparencies, a screen, videocassette player, television, computer, and multimedia projector. If these things are not immediately available, the college instructor can request them from an "AV" department. Unfortunately, in a field training setting, you may not have access to this equipment. Further, the field "classroom" could be inside a station or onboard a vehicle and not in a classroom. So, is familiarity with this equipment essential to the field training officer? If one of your responsibilities is to help with classroom or in-service training, then being familiar with these items is important. In addition, if you set up a "training unit" or designated station for training, then some of this equipment will be on-hand for your use.

Audiovisual aids in the teaching setting are numerous and include medical equipment and mannikins as well as educational equipment. Since you are familiar with the medical equipment and training mannikins, it is important to know about the audiovisial aids used in training. Depending on your agency's training budget, you may have a few of these items or most of them. The items include:

- *Chalkboard or dry erase board:* The chalkboard or dry erase board is a tool used to communicate to the trainees by writing the information onto the board. Write key words and not entire paragraphs.

- *Easel and pad:* In the absence of a chalkboard or dry erase board, you can use an easel and pad. Easel and pads are especially helpful if you want to keep the information for later reference during the training. If you attach a sheet of paper to a painted wall, be sure to use only masking tape or the wall will be marked or paint damaged.

- *Slide projector:* A 35-mm slide projector has been a staple of the training industry for years. More recently, however, it has given way to the laptop computer and portable multimedia projector.

- *Slides:* Shoes can visually emphasize key points.
- *Overhead projector:* Another staple of the training industry, this device can be used where a slide projector and slides cannot be used or are not available. Some multimedia projectors have a built-in video camera that can capture a printed handout and show it on the screen. This newer projector replaces the older "opaque" projector known under the brand name of Elmo.

- *Overhead transparencies:* Overhead transparencies not only can bring out key points, the instructor can write or draw on the overhead and provide additional information.
- *Computer:* Computers can make developing training materials such as slides and handouts much easier.

- *Multimedia projector:* This projector connects to a computer so that a slide presentation on the computer can be shown on a screen.

- *Screen:* Although not an absolute requirement for showing slides or overhead transparencies, it is helpful if you are in a well-lighted room and need a relflective surface or are in a room with no blank walls.

- *Videocassette player and television:* A number of agencies produce professional videotapes for continuing education. Also, your EMS agency may have videocameras to record calls or training sessions for later review.

There are a few things to keep in mind when using audiovisual equipment:

- If using a chalkboard, make sure chalk is available.
- If using a dry erase board, make sure the markers do not have a toxic solvent. Some markers release fumes which can be slightly intoxicating.
- When erasing a chalkboard or dry erase board, do not use any pattern (up–down or side to side) since the students' eyes will follow the eraser. An erratic pattern will keep them awake.

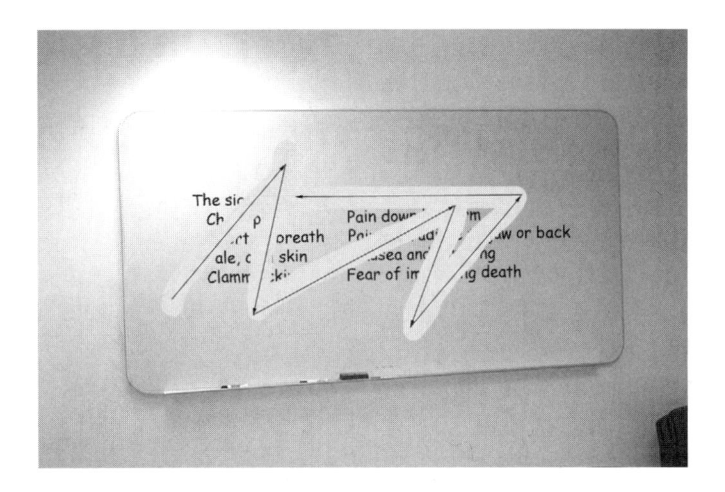

- If using slides, make sure they are in the tray correctly. Also, remember that a spare bulb is an essential tool.
- If using overheads, make sure you have a spare bulb.
- If using a VCR, make sure the tape has been rewound before playing.
- Be prepared to "wing it." Murphy (as in Murphy's law) works for you, too.

Since a field setting may not allow this equipment for your use, you will need to improvise. One essential item for the FTO is a notepad. First, the new employee can use the notepad to write questions for which an answer is not immediately available. Second, you can use the notepad to write information pertaining to the employee's performance. Finally, you can use the notepad as a substitute for the chalkboard or dry erase board. What is convenient about using the notepad as a "chalkboard" is that you can give the sheet(s) of paper to the trainee for future reference.

SUMMARY

Every profession has its tools, and training is one that has its own tools. The field training officer needs to be familiar with the equipment found in the classroom so that he or she can use it to enhance a training program. While most EMS agencies cannot afford all of the training aids, as the costs of the items drop, additional equipment may be acquired. Being familiar with the equipment at your disposal can mean less embarrassing moments when something goes wrong.

18

Another Role

The Field Training Officer as Performance Consultant

The following scene is common. A shift supervisor comes to you and tells you that he is sending John Doe to training. The supervisor complains that John is not doing his job and needs to be retrained. Since you are the training officer, you are to retrain him and bring him up to a satisfactory level. Then, when you meet with John to reiterate that he has been assigned to training, he reacts defiantly, nearly yelling about the supervisor's inability to manage, exclaiming, "What does *he* know about what I can do?" John tells you he feels that he is being sent to jail for something he didn't do. And he's right.

Too often training has been used as a form of punishment or as the first step in managing someone out of an organization. Or, there have been "shotgun" approaches to training—having training sessions for training sake—only to find out that the training session had very little impact in achieving an overall goal. Perhaps it is time to rethink these positions. The purpose of this chapter is to consider the field training officer's role as a performance consultant—one who confers with the client (in this case, the supervisor) to determine the real needs behind a request for training.

THE TIMES, THEY ARE A-CHANGING

Before continuing with the discussion on performance consulting, let us take a look at the role the field training officer has traditionally played. Often, a manager, supervisor, or commander will approach the field training officer and proclaim, "We need some training," and then launch into a monologue about what is needed. Dutifully, the field training officer will run off to construct the program, not knowing if what is being designed is what is really needed. To assess your role as a field training officer, read through the descriptions of the roles below and choose all that apply to your specific role. Choose the number of all of the statements that apply to your role as a trainer in EMS:

1. I identify and address the learning needs of the EMTs and paramedics within my agency.
2. I identify and address the performance needs of the EMTs and paramedics within my agency.
3. My primary role is to produce structured learning opportunities.
4. My primary role is to change or improve an EMT or paramedic's job performance.

5. Training is an end—if the EMTs and paramedics have learned something, I have been successful.
6. Training is a means to an end—when EMTs and paramedics use the information in their jobs, I have succeeded.
7. I am held accountable for the training activity. I am critiqued by the number of classes, the number of participants, and the number of hours I spend teaching.
8. I am held accountable for partnering with the supervisors and managers and continuing improvement of the EMTs' and paramedics' performance.
9. Course and program evaluations are completed by the participants and assess their reaction/ to the training they have received.
10. The level of performance improvement and cost–benefit to the agency is a key factor in assessing the value of the training program.
11. I assess the training needs of the employees in my agency.
12. I look for performance gaps and reasons for these gaps.
13. The training I conduct is viewed as a cost to the agency with a limited link to the agency's business goals.
14. The training I conduct is a service that has measurable goals, including, for example, cost savings. My training is highly linked to the goals of the organization.
15. When approached by a supervisor, manager, or commander and asked to conduct training on a specific topic, I quickly begin to develop the program.
16. When approached by a supervisor, manager, or commander and asked to conduct training on a specific topic, I consult with the person to determine performance gaps and the impact of the training on the EMS agency.

Scoring—Odd numbered statements reflect traditional trainer roles. Even numbered statements reflect the trainer role as a performance consultant. If you are in a traditional trainer role, you may be more like an order taker, fulfilling managements perceptions of training without knowing if the training is making an impact on performance. A field training officer may want to be more of an educational consultant—giving managers and field personnel what they need to do the job better.

PERFORMANCE CONSULTING

In performance consulting, the field training officer gets to the real need behind the request for training. Sometimes there is a gap in training that special classes can fill. Other times, the request for training is often the first indication of an underlying problem that has yet to be identified. More often, performance consulting identifies the problem and creates solutions or interventions for it, such as training, outsourcing, partnering, or otherwise influencing a behavioral change. Ultimately, on-the-job performance will be enhanced. As an example, consider the following exchange:

Supervisor: John doesn't know how to apply a traction splint. We need to send him to training to relearn how to apply the splint.

Training officer: OK, I will get him into training as soon as I can. Let me check the schedule.

The above dialogue has accomplished nothing. According to the supervisor, John has a deficiency. What has the supervisor observed to lead him to that conclusion? The training officer, in a servile role, agrees to put John into refresher training without really knowing if there is a true need for it. A different dialogue might sound like the following:

Supervisor:	John doesn't know how to apply a traction splint. We need to send him to training to relearn how to apply the splint.
Training officer:	What part of the skill does John not know how to perform?
Supervisor:	I dunno. All of it, I guess. He seemed to have messed it up on a call that I monitored the other day.
Training officer:	Were there factors that prevented him from doing the skill the way you thought it should be done?
Supervisor:	No. None that I could see.
Training officer:	Is it that John can't perform the skill or because he didn't want to?
Supervisor:	What do you mean?
Training officer:	Have you seen him apply a traction splint before? If you brought him in here right now to show you how this is done, could he do it correctly?
Supervisor:	Well, yeah, I have seen him do it—he can apply the traction splint.
Training officer:	Have you spoken to John about what you observed?
Supervisor:	Yes. I told him he really screwed up and needs to go to training.
Training officer:	Based upon what you have told me—your observation that he knows how to apply a traction splint since you've seen him do this before—this isn't a training problem. Rather, it appears to be a behavioral issue. You may want to address the issue with John directly.

Yes, There Is a New Way

The key is consulting with the supervisor to find out the root cause of the problem and why there is a perceived need for training. In the above exchange, the training officer did not concede that John needed training. In questioning the supervisor, it was revealed that John does know how to do the skill but chose not to perform it correctly on that specific call. There may have been other factors affecting John's performance. What was the supervisor's role and demeanor at the scene? Did John perform the skill in a manner that was unacceptable to the supervisor? These questions, and others like it, will help the training officer get the information he or she needs to determine the need for training and its end result.

The Client, Sponsor, Customer

Before getting into the steps involved in performance consulting, it is important to look at a few things that are different from the way the training officer now performs the job. First, the training officer must rethink the job description—to be a consultant as well as a trainer. While the work of designing and implementing training programs will be the same, the process of determining what classes will be offered is different.

Second, instead of having an employer, field supervisors, and employees, the training officer will have sponsors, clients, and customers. The sponsor is usually the agency that employs the training officer. The client and sponsor can be the same. In the example used above, the supervisor is the client. Could the supervisor also be the sponsor? Possibly, but typically the sponsor is the one who will pay for or fund the training. The customer is the person participating in the training—the EMT or paramedic working for the service.

Steps in Performance Consulting

There are eight steps in performance consulting (see the table below). These steps include Entry, Scoping, Initial Contracting, Diagnosis, Feedback, Contract, Intervention (i.e., training), and Impact. In each of these steps, the training officer will consult with the client who is requesting the training to help determine any gaps in performance. The training officer and client will work together to identify the best way to resolve the gaps. After consulting with the client, there will, on occasion, be no actual need to develop and implement a training program.

Performance Consulting Steps

Phase	Questions	Preferred Outcomes
Entry Initial contact.	What are you seeing? What are managers seeing? What are managers requesting?	Develop an entry statement. Set a reason for the meeting.
Scoping Assess the problem for the EMS agency and its impact.	What are the signs/symptoms of the problem? What is the problem for the EMS agency? What is the cost or impact of the problem? What is the perceived performance? What is the desired performance? What are the drivers of performance? What are the perceived performance gaps?	Define the problem. Focus the manager on the problem instead of the immediate solution.
Initial Contract Assess the need/desire to further investigate and diagnose versus wait and watch.	What initial actions are needed? What should be explored further? What are the conditions of contract—who does what and when?	Manager owns the problem. Manager owns subsequent steps. Maintain objectivity.
Diagnosis Collect data, explore performance drivers, and analyze data.	What is the actual performance versus desired performance? What are the likely causes of performance gaps? What are the drivers of performance?	The field training officer understands performance drivers and the context of the problem.
Feedback Present data and explore possible interventions, consider cost–benefit.	What does the diagnosis indicate? What do the field training officer and manager consider as causes of performance gaps? What can be done about it (joint ideas)?	Let data speak for itself. Keep the manager as owner of the problem. Manager understands performance drivers. Further explore need.
Contract Make verbal agreement, followed by e-mail or written agreement.	What actions should be taken? Is the cost–benefit reasonable? What are conditions of contract—who does what and when?	Role and expectations are defined. Develop the project plan. Partner with the manager. Return on investment is discussed.
Intervention Provide training.	Is training working as planned? Is communication effective? Are there other opportunities?	Implement training. Is field training officer and manager involved with project management.
Business Impact Monitor performance drivers and look at return on investment.	Did the training address performance gaps? Did the training meet the cost–benefit expectations? Did the training identify other performance gaps?	Look at return on investment. Analyze the effectiveness of training. Analyze the impact on overall function of the EMS agency.

The initial step in the consultation process is **Entry.** At this stage, someone who feels that there is a training need (the client) contacts the training officer. During this step, it is important to determine what the client sees as a need. Questions should be tailored to identify the need as the client sees it. In the case of the traction splint, the following questions could be asked:

- What seems to be the problem?
- What happened to cause you to call me?
- Why do you think there is a problem?
- What do you think we need to do?

These questions start the consultation process in motion. They invite the client to think about the person's on-the-job performance or how they would like the person to perform the job. They also ask the client what they think needs to be done to remedy the problem. During this stage, it is important not to agree to any form of training, since no clear need for training has been established.

The training officer can also initiate this process. For example, if the training officer accompanies a crew on a call and identifies a need for training, Entry has begun.

- What did the training officer see?
- What would the training officer like to see (specifically)?
- What can be done to remedy the problem?

After Entry into the consultation, **Scoping** begins. Questions in this step are centered on the symptoms of the problem, the desired and perceived performance, and the possible gaps in the performance that might exist. This is a great opportunity for brainstorming, especially in performance gaps that are complex. Sample questions during Scoping might include:

- What part of the splinting process did you feel was incorrect?
- Was the attempt different than the procedure documented in textbooks? If so, how was it different?
- What happened when the EMT attempted to use the traction splint?
- Did the splint work?
- What impact did this have on the patient?
- What were you able to identify as the problem with the procedure?
- Did you observe any behavior that got in the way of applying the traction splint?

Occasionally, the training officer will meet with resistance from the client. This is especially true the first few times the client wants to dump an issue onto the training department's doorstep. The client may become irritated and refuse to answer questions. This is not the time to agree to take over the problem and provide something just to placate the client. For example, consider the following exchange:

Supervisor:	I don't have time for this nonsense. You're the training officer, you handle it.
Training officer:	I'm sorry. No. Based upon what we've talked about [reiterate the key points using the clients' words], training wouldn't be the solution you are looking for. It may be that there are other issues such as [state possible issues] that are contributing to how John is performing on the job. If that is the case, then it would be more appropriate for you to handle the situation.

With this approach, the evidence speaks for the consultant. The consultant stays objective, professional, and nonpersonal in response (so the client isn't offended by the "No, I won't do it" response). The consultant states a conclusion that the client might not want to hear; however, the consultant also gives the client something—suggestions about where the problem could be—and keeps ownership of the problem with the client.

In addition, it might be appropriate to ask what the client has done about the perceived problem. While a problem does exist, the client just does not know its root cause. For example, consider the following questions:

- Have you spoken with John about the problem?
- Does he know what he did wrong?
- Have you told John about your meeting with me?

After Scoping, it would be appropriate to enter into an **Initial Contract.** In this phase, the training officer and client determine if there is a need to diagnose the problem further. A decision is made as to whether to wait and see or to treat the symptoms at this time. It is also important not to take ownership of the problem. The client owns it, not the training officer.

The initial contract will identify the steps that will be taken after the initial meeting. Things to consider for the initial contract include further exploration if necessary, who will perform the exploration, any steps to be taken in diagnosing or correcting the problem, and who will be responsible for specific tasks. Again, it is imperative that the client retains ownership of the problem. The initial contract will also set a date and time to continue the consultation. The date does not have to be weeks in the future. It could be as soon as the next shift. Along with a follow-up date, the initial contract may contain information on:

- The next steps to be taken
- Any boundaries to the analysis or diagnosis to include the nature of the data gathering, such as interviews, review of patient care reports, and other steps
- The overall objectives of the work to be accomplished and the kind of information to be researched
- The role of the training officer, client, and any other colleagues or partners in the project
- Mutual status checks on the progress of everyone involved
- What the training officer will present at the end of the evaluation
- An agreement of confidentiality.

It is not necessary to enter into a formal contract in which everything is written and signed. Rather, the initial contract can be agreed upon verbally with a follow-up e-mail sent to the client.

If additional steps are to be taken, the next level is **Diagnosis** of the problem. At this time, additional information is gathered to identify the specific gaps in performance. The training officer and client should work together to answer the following questions:

- What is the actual performance being demonstrated?
- How does this compare with the desired performance?
- What performance gaps most likely exist?
- Are there any behaviors that affect performance?
- Are there outside influences (away from the job) affecting performance?

After the information has been gathered, the follow-up meeting will be used for the next level—**Feedback.** The information will be discussed, along with possible interventions. Questions to be considered at this level include:

- What does the information show?
- Are the data indicating a performance gap?
- What do the training officer and client think are causes of the performance gap? (Note that this is a joint discovery process.)
- What ideas have the training officer and client developed to correct the problem? (Again, note that this is a collaborative effort.)

When giving feedback, communication with the client needs to be objective, based on the data or information collected. Refrain from any emotions and remain businesslike throughout the meeting. Be engaged and involved in the conversation, using appropriate body language to convey interest.

After feedback, a plan of action is developed. The actions to be taken along with the solution are considered to be the **Contract** level of the consultation. As with the initial contract, the contract is the final agreement between the training officer and client, and defines each person's roles and responsibilities. It also highlights the plan for intervention and the level of performance to be achieved. It will also include any outsourcing or partnering with a subject matter expert if needed. If any costs will be incurred, the contract also needs to specify who will be responsible for covering the expenses. For example, if an option is to send John to a refresher course, then the fees for the course need to be paid by someone. Does training, operations, or John pay the fees?

Like the initial contract, no formal, written agreement is needed. Verbal contracting with an e-mail follow-up should suffice. The e-mail reiterates the components of the contract and assures that everyone is in agreement.

After the contract has been agreed upon, the **Intervention** level begins. Intervention includes what type of action is going to be taken by the consultant and management to remedy the problem. This may involve the design of a training session. It also includes implementing the training, coordinating the subject matter experts, arranging logistics, facilitating, and addressing other gaps discovered. If the consultant is also the facilitator of the training, then an additional gap may become apparent, requiring follow-up and/or training in other areas as necessary.

In the case of the errant splint, a possible intervention might be to set up a one-on-one training session at a time that is convenient for John as well as the training officer. If the supervisor wants to be present, a convenient time for the supervisor should also be considered. Note that the training officer and supervisor are both involved in developing the intervention.

After the intervention, last level of the consultation, **Impact,** occurs. Impact involves monitoring the training to see if there has been a return on investment: Did the time and money spent on the project achieve the results desired? Feedback from the participant(s) in the form of a written survey can get information from only the classroom perspective. But participant evaluations do not always indicate that the goal has been achieved. It will be necessary to follow up with the client to determine if there was a change in performance. The follow-up can be used to assure the client's support of the training—assuring that the client agreed with the training and that it is beneficial to the participant or participants involved. In the example, a follow-up with the supervisor would include asking if he or she had observed John using the traction splint and if John had applied the device correctly. The consultant can take an active role in influencing the transfer of skills learned in the classroom to the job. By putting a follow-up plan in place with management, management will be an active part of the change in performance.

PERFORMANCE CONSULTING GOES BEYOND PROBLEM SOLVING

What about the other dilemma training officers face—having training for the sake of training, in essence, sponsoring a class without knowing if there is a specific need for the program? Consider receiving this request from one of the EMTs in a basic life-support ambulance service: "We need training in reading ECGs." The training officer, looking for ideas, might think, "Wow, great idea" and begin getting things together. But is this an appropriate need-to-know skill for a basic life-support service? Using performance consulting concepts, the training officer may determine there is no need for ECG training since no benefit (enhanced customer service) will be realized by the ambulance service.

In contrast, the training officer may find that a large number of EMTs would like to know the skill. Then the question arises: Will the skill be beneficial to the ambulance service? When will the skill be used? The answer could be that the skill won't be used.

The problem here is that the training officer's customers or students would be the EMTs; however, the sponsor of the training program would be the ambulance service. Key questions to consider before offering such a class would be:

- Would the new skills be reinforced on the job?
- Would the new skills be a component of the EMT's job performance evaluation?
- Would the ambulance service benefit from the EMTs having this skill?

In assessing the value of the training, the answer to each of the questions above would be no. Thus, while holding a class in reading ECGs sounds like fun and would enhance the EMTs' knowledge base, it would serve no purpose to the ambulance service or benefit it. It would be the training officer's discretion to offer an ECG class, realizing that it would probably not bring much benefit to the company.

Performance consulting is also appropriate when the head of the ambulance service approaches the training officer with a list of classes and announces, "Here, we need this training over the next six months." Without being rude or becoming a servant to the boss, the training officer can begin the consulting process to completely assess if there really is a need for the sessions.

SUMMARY

As a training officer you wear a number of hats—instructor, facilitator, coach, father/mother confessor, counselor, and others—and that number has just gotten bigger. Performance consulting is the new direction of training and leads the way to productive, meaningful, and well-directed training programs. Initially, undertaking this role can be tedious and met with resistance. However, over the long run, there will be a better focus on the precise training needs with better results. The field training officer will find that, with time, resistance decreases as the benefits of performance consulting begin to pay off. This chapter has given you some insights into performance consulting that you can use on the job and make the training programs more effective.

19

Developing Your Training Session

Goals, Objectives, and Lesson Plans

If you don't know where you're going, you wind up someplace else!

Unlike the instructor at the community college or vocational–technical center, there is often no predetermined lesson plan for the field training officer to use. Although the EMS agency may conduct EMT refresher training that has a preset curriculum, many field training officers will have to develop continuing education or remedial training programs on their own. The purpose of this chapter is to give the field training officer information on developing a program that is unique to the EMS agency and one that meets the needs of the service and its employees.

STEPS IN DESIGNING YOUR TRAINING PROGRAM

Program design is a special process that involves many steps. Perhaps one of the best references for instructional design is the text *The Systematic Design of Instruction,* by Walter Dick, Lou Carey, and James Carey. In the text is a diagram that illustrates the process of developing a program (see illustration). For the inexperienced instructor, many of the terms can be intimidating, but once explained are easy to understand.

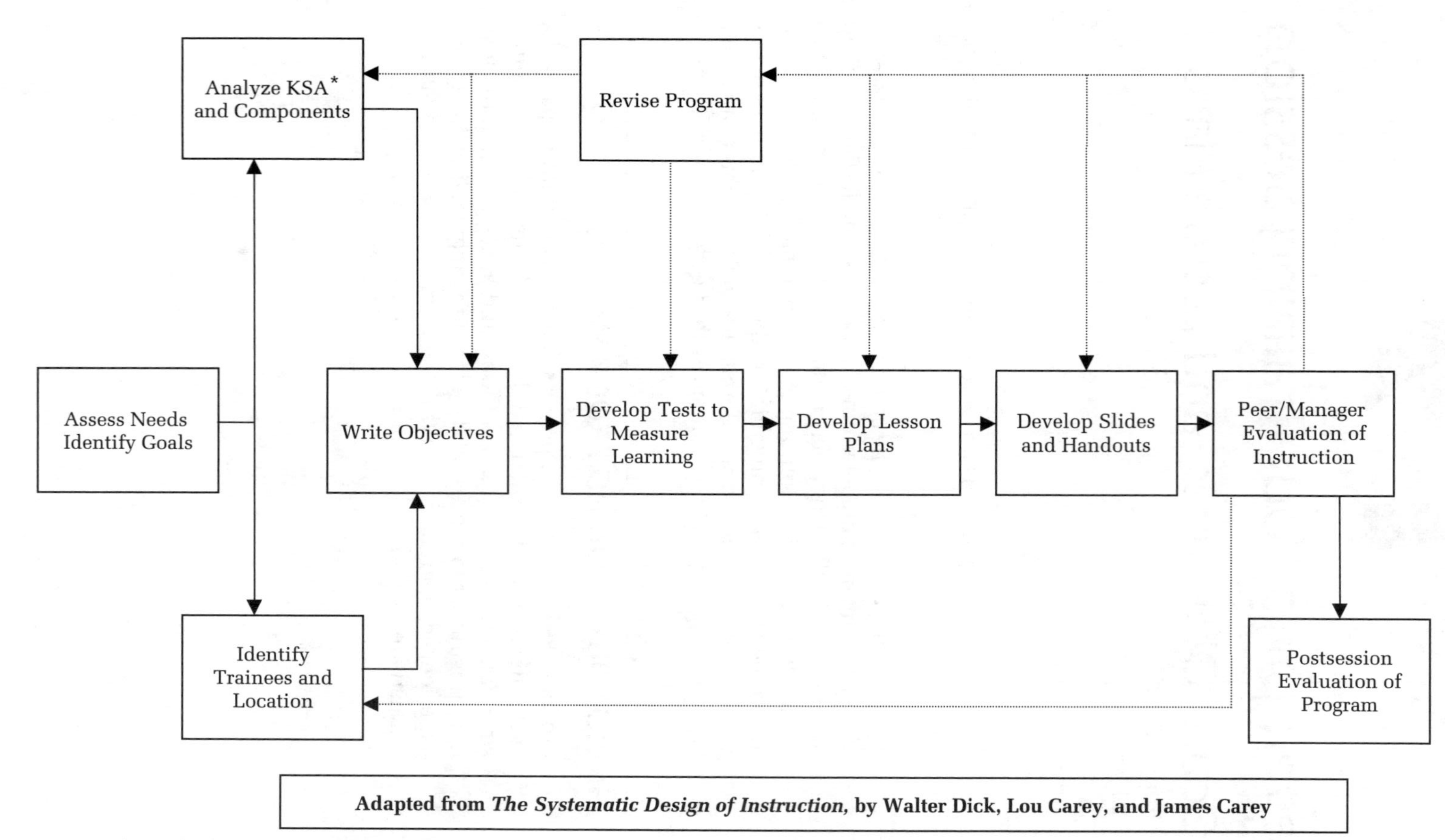

Adapted from *The Systematic Design of Instruction*, by Walter Dick, Lou Carey, and James Carey

* KSA—knowledge, skills, and attitudes

Assessing Training Needs and Identifying Goals

Whenever you are asked to develop a training program, the first step is to determine if there is a need for it. Perform a needs analysis. The diagram below illusrates a simple way of identifying a need for training.

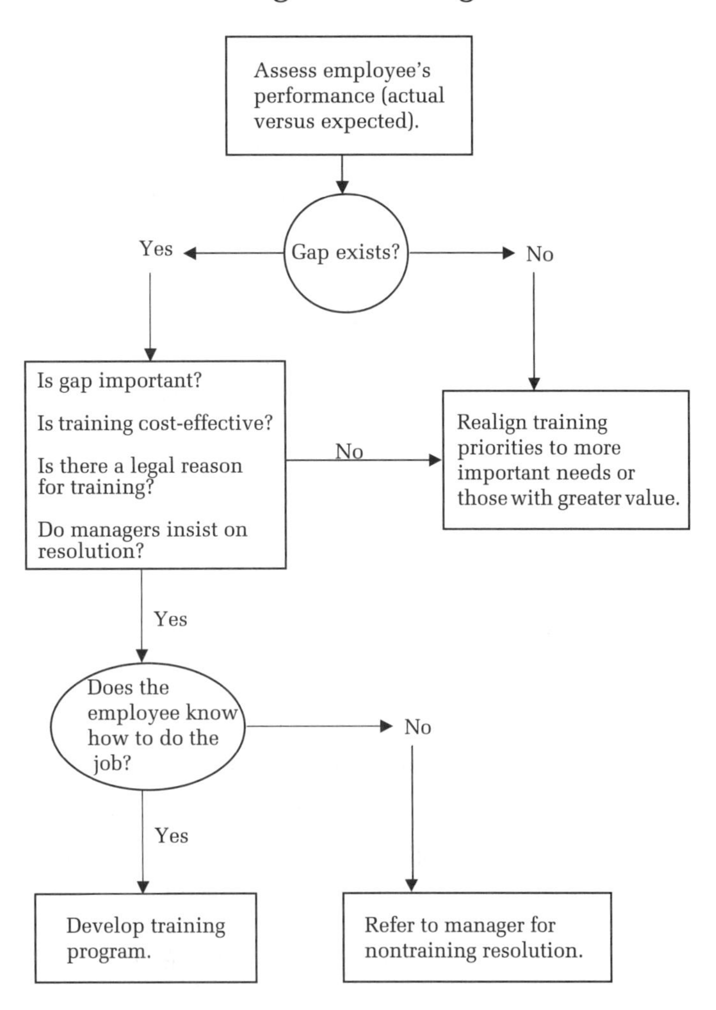

A training need can be identified in several situations—if an employee has demonstrated poor performance or when an EMS agency is faced with new equipment, policies, rules, regulations, or laws. If these reasons are minor or the cost of training would be exhorbitant, then the identified need may be assigned a lower priority. Another consideration is if the employee knows how to do the job. If the employee does have the basic knowledge, skills, and attitude to perform the job, then continuing education or remedial training would be appropriate. In contrast, if the employee does not have the basic knowledge, skill, or attitude to do the job, then the field training officer should refer the employee to the shift supervisor or commander for resolution.

Once a training need has been identified, the field training officer proceeds to identify goals and objectives. In addition, the field training officer will need to identify exactly what skills and components of those skills needs to be taught (instructional analysis) and determine who will participate in the session along with where the training will be conducted (the learners and context).

Goals and Objectives

When identifying a need for training, a general goal may quickly be established. However, as the program evolves, a more refinend goal may be created. Simply stated, a goal and objective means stating where you are going and how you will get there. As was briefly mentioned in the "Management" section, companies, including EMS agencies, need goals and objectives. In other words, companies need a plan or course of direction and a way of determining if the plan is successful. The same is true in education. If you don't have a plan, you will have no idea where you will end up. In education, as in management, these are called goals and objectives.

A goal is a general statement describing the end point of the training session. An objective is one part of the steps needed to achieve a goal. To be sure of where you are going, goals and objectives must be written. In preparing a goal, keep in mind that the goal is a general statement describing the end results of the learning process, that is, what you want the student to learn. The goal should include:

- Approximately when the end result will be achieved (At the end of the program . . .)
- Who will be affected by the goal (. . . *the employee, student, participant* . . .)
- A general idea of how the end result will be achieved (. . . will be trained in the . . .)
- The end result. (topic, skill.)

Assume you are responsible for developing an orientation program for newly hired employees that will have a session on the company's policies and procedures. In putting together and looking at the goal— "At the end of the orientation program, the new employee will be familiar with the policies and procedures of EMS Co."—there is very little in that statement that can be finitely measured to determine the new employee's proficiency in the company's policies and procedures. This goal does not state specific policies and procedures; rather, it refers to all policies and procedures used by the agency. However, objectives can be written to help meet the overall goal.

Once the goal has been written and the end result clearly identified, objectives to help meet the goal can be written. An objective is a clear and precise statement of what is to be achieved. An objective is also measurable in that it states how and how well the step or task is to be completed. An easy way to remember how to construct an objective is by using the acronym SMART. Each objective shuld be **S**pecific, **M**easurable, **A**ttainable, **R**elevant, and **T**rackable. Thus, the FTO can evaluate the new employee's performance based upon the objectives for either specific knowledge or a particular skill. There are a few points to keep in mind about objectives:

- They can be tedious.
- They can be repetitive.
- They can be difficult to write.

However, once written, objectives are an effective tool for measuring the degree of proficiency the employee has attained. When writing an objective, it must be specific, covering one particular piece of knowledge or one particular skill. It must also contain the way it can be measured so if it becomes part of the evaluation process, there is no room to question what is being asked and to what level the student must achieve. A breakdown of the contents of an objective for the policy and procedure training session mentioned above is as follows:

When the objective will be met (*At the end of the orientation program . . .*)
Who will be affected by the goal (*. . . the new employee . . .*)
How the end result will be achieved (*. . . will be able to . . .*)
A specific method by which the student will show his or her abilities (*list, state, demonstrate, define, discuss . . .*)
The specific knowledge or skill. (*e.g., the procedure for calling in sick.*)

Thus, one objective that helps meet the goal is:

> At the end of the orientation program, the new employee will be able to state the procedure for calling in sick."

If the new employee cannot state the procedure for calling in sick, he or she does not meet the objective.

Here is another objective:

> At the end of the orientation program, the new employee will be able to list the paid holidays authorized by the company.

Like the previous objective, there is specific information required, besides how well the employee is to perform. However, is the information critical to the new employee? If he or she cannot list all of the paid holidays, does it mean he or she is incompetent? The answer to both of these questions is no. But the objective can be "tightened up" to allow for some minor discrepancies in the new employee's knowledge. A reworded objective might be:

> At the end of the orientation program, the new employee will be able to list eight of the ten paid holidays authorized by the company.

Again, the objective contains the necessary components of who, what, how, and how well. But it gives the new employee some leeway in not being able to list all of the paid holidays. Thus, if the new employee can list eight, nine, or ten of the paid holidays, he or she has met the objective.

Objectives need to be written to cover the information that you want the person to learn. After the objectives have been developed, the lesson plan is created.

The Lesson Plan

This point is where this text differs from the diagram on instructional design. According to Dick, Carey, and Carey, the trainer should develop evalation tools before creating an instructional strategy (lesson plan) and materials (handouts, and so forth). Although you may or may not be giving lectures or classroom presentations, as a field training officer you should be familiar with the lesson plan. While objectives will tell you what the trainee needs to know to successfully complete the program, the lesson plan will be your guide to get you from beginning to end. The lesson plan can be a detailed outline of the topics to be covered during a particular section of the program, or a lesson plan could be a detailed presentation guide that includes important talking points. Refer to Appendix A for examples of each type of lesson plan.

Why are goals, objectives, and lesson plans necessary? As an experienced EMT or paramedic, you have a wealth of knowledge and experience. To impart this information, it needs to be organized and presented in a logical sequence. Further, it sets a standard for all employees to be taught the same thing even though there may be different instructors teaching the material. Often, a new employee will be assigned to several field training officers during the orientation program. This can be attributed, in part, to shift schedules, vacations, illness, and other valid reasons.

SUMMARY

Each field training officer has a way of doing some things in the field which can be different from the other field training officers. However, this can be confusing to the new employee: "If Joe does it this way, Anne this other way, and Fred's technique is totally different, then who is right?" Chances are, they are all correct. But the trainee is lost. If he or she performs a skill for Anne that Joe taught and Anne fails the trainee, the new employee has a legitimate complaint. The task of instructional design, from objectives to lesson plan to evaluations, can standardize what is taught, when it is taught, and the degree of proficiency the trainee must achieve. This chapter has reviewed the basic priniciples of instructional design so that the field training officer understands the complexities of designing a course of instruction for the EMS agency employees.

20

Developing Post-Training Performance Assessment Tools

In addition to developing goals, objectives, and lesson plans, a field training officer must develop an assessment tool to determine if learning has taken place—a test of the employee's knowledge. Without a means of assessing if learning has occurred, the field training officer may have no indication of the success of the program.

In addition, the field training officer may also have to critique a new employee's initial performance or assist with an employee's annual performance review. The purpose of this chapter is to discuss developing assessment tools that will help evaluate learning and that can be used in a new employee or annual performance review.

THE EVALUATION PROCESS

Evaluating the employee's knowledge and skill proficiency can be accomplished by several methods. Assessments are based upon the objectives for the class, with test questions developed accordingly. There are several methods for evaluating knowledge:

- True–false questions
- Matching questions
- Multiple-choice questions
- Oral examinations
- Short-answer questions
- Short-essay questions
- Essays
- Practical skills examinations

Written test questions can be difficult to develop, especially multiple-choice items. The nature of any written examination needs to be based on the information to be tested, degree of difficulty, number of questions to be asked, and the length of time needed to grade the exam. While multiple choice tests are more difficult to build, they are the easiest and most objective to grade. In contrast, essay tests are relatively easy to develop but can consume a lot of time to grade.

The most commonly used test format is multiple choice. When writing a multiple choice question, there are few key points to remember:

- The initial part of the question is called the premise or stem. It contains enough information to allow the student to begin formulating an answer. Avoid a premise such as "Which of the following is true?" It is permissible to word the question, "Which of the following statements is correct when treating a patient in insulin shock?"

- The "answers" are called distractors. Typical multiple-choice questions consist of the premise and four distractors, one of which is the correct answer. Each question should contain the same number of distractors. Typically, multiple-choice questions contain four distractors. If you write a question with a fifth distractor (usually the correct answer), special attention will be paid to that extra distractor and the question may not be a valid measurement. All distractors should be about the same length across the page. A very long distractor stands out and is probably worded to make it correct. Again, it tends to invalidate the question. Distractors should also be believable so that, if the trainee does not know the correct answer, he or she may choose an incorrect one because it "sounds right."
- Avoid using "None of the above." Some tests use that as a distractor on numerous questions. To some, it appears as if the test writer could not think of a plausible answer and used "None of the above" as filler.
- Avoid using qualifier words such as *always* or *never*. It is a giveaway that the answer is incorrect.
- Scatter the correct answers among the distractors. Do not have most of the correct answers in distractor B or D.

Here are some examples of poor and good multiple choice questions:

Poor Multiple Choice Questions

Q. All of the following are true except:
  a. A quick scene survey is important to determine safety.
  b. Announce your arrival at the scene on the PA system.
  c. Promptly locate the patient and begin patient assessment.
  d. None of the above—all are true.

  Bad premise, since the reader has no idea what the question is asking. Use of "None of the above" is not good.

Q. Patient assessment begins with:
  a. Assessing vital signs.
  b. Performing a neurological check.
  c. Checking for level of consciousness, airway, breathing, and pulse.
  d. Conducting a head-to-toe survey.

  Premise is fair, but answer C is much longer than the others and becomes very obvious.

Better Multiple Choice Questions

Q. Upon arriving at the scene of the call, you will do several important things. Which of the following steps would you NOT do upon arriving at the scene of a call?
  a. Perform a quick scene survey to determine safety.
  b. Notify the dispatcher of your arrival at the scene.
  c. Promptly locate the patient and begin assessment.
  d. Fill out the address of the call on your trip report.

  Premise poses the question. Note the capitalized word that emphasizes the negative. Distractors are plausible and all about the same length.

Q. Patient assessment begins with the primary survey that consists of:
  a. Assessing the patient's vital signs.
  b. Performing a neurological check.
  c. Assessing LOC and the ABCs.
  d. Conducting a head-to-toe survey.

  Premise poses the question. Distractors are plausible and the same length.

As for other tests, such as true–false, matching, short answer, and oral exams, some general principles will help you develop effective measurements:

- As with multiple-choice items, true–false questions should avoid words like *always* and *never.*
- For matching test questions, have one or two more answers than questions.
- Short-answer or fill-in-the-blank questions should be direct and not subject to interpretation.
- Avoid too many blanks in fill-in-the-blank questions. The trainee needs to know what is being asked!
- Short essay and essay questions are subject to interpretation by the trainee and, thus, subject to being challenged. The field training officer may have to allow for variations in answers for these types of questions.
- When conducting an oral or verbal exam, avoid using phrases like "In your experience" or "In your opinion." If you use such a phrase, it does not matter what the answer is, since the answer is always correct!

Keys to an Effective Skills Evaluation

Most often, a field training officer will be assessing the employee's performance or skill proficiency. Evaluating skill performance is a more difficult process because it is subjective and can be influenced by the evaluator's knowledge, abilities, and feelings. When evaluating the employee's skills, keep in mind several important things:

- Evaluate the skill or knowledge, not the person.
- Find something good and not focus only on the errors.
- Be fair.
- Be honest.
- Keep your emotions or personal feelings about the new employee out of the evaluation process.
- Do not expect the new employee to perform the skill the way you do.
- Do not expect the new employee to perform the skill at demonstration level.
- Do not compare one employee with any other employee.

A helpful tool is the skill evaluation sheet. The skill evaluation sheet lists the steps the new employee needs to complete in order to pass the skill. Not only does it list all the steps, it also indicates which steps are critical. If an employee does not complete a critical part of the skill, he or she does not pass the skill no matter how well all other steps are performed. Critical performance errors are those which risk the safety of the person performing the skill or the health and safety of the person on whom the skill is being used. For example, in performing CPR, if the trainee does not check for breathing and/or does not ventilate the "patient," he or she fails the skill and must repeat it.

A benefit to the skills evaluation sheet is the objectivity it offers. Either the new employee does or does not perform the step. Each step of the skill is scored and, if the skill is done correctly, the new employee passes. Another benefit is that the new employee has a written record of his or her performance and can see the good things as well as errors. Samples of skills evaluation sheets can be found in Appendix B.

The field training officer may be responsible for conducting or assisting with a performance evaluation review (PER) on new employees or having input into a PER on existing employees. The PER is a written evaluation tool that, once completed, becomes a part of the employee's personnel record to show growth in the job or the need for improvement. The PER is used to determine proficiency in company policies, procedures, and skills, as well as assess the new employee's readiness to be assigned to a shift and new partner.

Your EMS agency might already have a performance evaluation review in place. Be sure you are familiar with the tool and understand the scoring for each area. To help your agency modify its PER or develop another form, a sample PER is included in Appendix C. The PER consists of several sections, including:

- Professional appearance
- Operations procedures and equipment use
- Demonstrated driving ability
- Employee standards
- Patient care
- Documentation

On the sample PER, each section is to be completed and signed by the FTO. Each area has numeric scores as well as space for written comments. An important concept in evaluating employees is the mechanism by which a score is determined. In the sample PER, you will note a page detailing what each numeric score represents. This information should be shared with the employee so that he or she knows how scores will be determined. While there is considerable room for a subjective evaluation, there needs to be consistency in scoring. Without scoring standards, it would be very difficult to critique an employee's abilities.

Typically for new employees, the field training officer reviews each section of the PER with the new employee at the end of the orientation period. The field training officer discusses the new employee's strengths and weaknesses, offering suggestions for improvement. The new employee reviews the PER with the field training officer and signs it. Once completed, the PER is given to management for review.

If the new employee is ready to be assigned to a regular shift, the new employee will be given a duty assignment after the PER has been completed. If the new employee is in need of additional training and orientation, the field training officer will make that recommendation to the training and operations divisions, which will arrange for additional on-the-road time with a different field training officer.

If, after being assigned to a second field training officer for additional training, the new employee is still in need of training, a decision will be made as to whether the new employee is trainable or whether the employee and company should end their relationship.

SUMMARY

This chapter has presented information about assessing the effectiveness of the training that was presented as well as conducting a performance evaluation review on new or veteran employees. To determine if an employee has retained any of the information presented during a training session, it is necessary to evaluate the knowledge and, if appropriate, the skills learned. Written and skills tests must be carefully crafted to be as fair and as objective as possible, assessing the trainee based upon the objectives of the program. In addition, the field training officer may be called upon to assist in an annual performance evaluation review for existing employees. To be fair and objective, criteria and a scoring mechanism must be developed.

21

Dazzling with Brilliance

Developing Your Presentation

In the previous chapters, we discussed identifying training needs, developing goals, objectives and lesson plans, and creating tools for measuring knowledge and skills. The next step is to design your presentation—another component of instructional strategies. This chapter will focus on making your presentation into one that the EMTs and paramedics will enjoy as well as one that will be educational.

IN THE BEGINNING

You have been asked to develop a program for the EMS agency that will train employees on a new, important topic. You have plenty of references and subject matter, but need to deliver the information in a concise and timely manner. When initially crafting your presentation, you need to consider several things:

- What do you and your organization want to achieve?
- What are the goals and objectives?
- What do you want the participants to take away from the presentation?
- What attitude do you want the participants to have at the end of your presentation?
- Look at the message you will be delivering and determine its nature—is it positive, negative, persuasive?

Once you have answered these questions, you can then determine how your presentation will look and what "props" you will need to reinforce your topic. The props include:

- Slides
- Handouts for use during or after the presentation

Your Slides

After developing your goals and objectives, you will need to prepare some visual aids to help get your point across. Many people are visual learners, meaning that they learn best when seeing the information on a screen or by watching the instructor. An excellent tool to develop your slides is Microsoft's PowerPoint or

Apple's Keynote software. You can develop your slides or overhead transparencies using the software, then print the slides on overhead transparencies and have them printed on 35mm slides, or use the computer and a multimedia projector to show them. In addition, PowerPoint can print your slides on a handout so that the participants can have a copy of the slides for later reference.

Theme

In developing your slide presentation, consider a theme and basic design when creating slides. The theme of the presentation is the context of the information that attracts the participants' attention and is something they will find particularly compelling. Go over the reference materials and look for key words or phrases that are repeated often and use those words or phrases as your theme. Repeating those words or phrases reinforces learning.

Give your slides and presentation an attention-getting title—something that will pique the curiosity of the EMTs and paramedics who will attend. When you come up with a title, you may want to get the input of your colleagues to determine if the title is appealing. An example might be a presentation on herbal remedies that the field crews might encounter. A title that has been used is "How Does Your Garden Grow: Herbal Remedies Encountered in the Field." Sometimes coming up with a unique title is difficult, and you might need to resort to a simple phrase that is a descriptive term of the content. An example might be, "Stress Management."

Basic Design

PowerPoint has several templates that you can use to design your slides. Templates contain the basic design elements that you will need in the creation of your slide presentation. While the purpose of this discussion is not a PowerPoint tutorial, it is important for you to know that the software makes it easy for the beginner. Be sure to look at the templates and, if you find one that meets your needs, use it. Otherwise, you will need to develop your own master slide. You need to consider any graphics that you might want to use, along with any agency logos and colors.

Text Type

The text on your presentation should be legible from the back of the room; thus, the type size should be large. Vary the type size to emphasize points, keeping the large type for the more important points. Limit the number of fonts, sizes, and weights. While some of the fancy fonts may look great on your computer screen, they may be hard to read at a distance. Use sans serif fonts for ease of reading, and avoid using all capital letters or underlining for emphasis. Type that is all capitalized is difficult to read and looks as if you are yelling. Rather, for emphasis, use a bold type or change the color.

Colors

Adding color is an important aspect of your slides, and it can set or break a mood. If you are using a PowerPoint template, a color scheme is associated with it. You can change or add to the scheme depending on your needs. Your text color needs to be distinctive from your background color. Remember that color-blind people have a hard time seeing greens and reds. If you use too much green or red color combinations, those individuals will not be able to read your slides.

You should consider primary and complementary colors. On a color wheel, primary colors (red, yellow, and blue) are located opposite their complementary colors (green, orange, and purple). Using complementary colors enhances the visual appeal of your presentation.

As was previously mentioned, the choice of color can have a significant impact on the mood of your presentation. Here are some hints on color selection:

Background colors—blue, green, and purple—are "cool" colors

- Blue is popular for business presentations and invites peace, contemplation, patience, and competence.
- Green seeks participation from the audience. It is restful and refreshing and indicates harmony, growth, money, and relaxation.
- Purple is impressive and could be seen as spiritual. Keep purple, especially light purple, to a minimum, as it can be distracting.

Foreground colors—red, orange, and yellow—are "warm" colors

- Red is a hot and dominating color that calls attention to your message and invites the audience to take action. It is a good color to use for emphasis.
- Orange is a great color for contrast, especially in your text. It tends to be powerful, yet cheerful and stimulates communication.
- Yellow stimulates the brain and promotes decision making. It is an excellent color for emphasis and tends to be bright, cheerful, and enthusiastic. Refrain from using yellow in a large room, as it may not be easily seen from the back of the room.

White and black are also safe colors to use. Be careful when using white, however, since the slide may be too bright for a small room and perceived as harsh on the eyes.

Formatting Information

After choosing your template and color scheme, it is time to begin putting the information onto the slides. Organize your slides by subtopic, using the subtopic title as the header on the slide. For each slide, follow some basic rules that will enhance your presentation:

- Use bullets to list your comments.
- Use an outline-type format.
- Do not write the entire speech onto the slide.
- Use no more than six to eight lines per slide, allowing no more than six to eight words per line.
- Use similar verb tenses and same number (singular or plural), that is, "is/are" and "was/were."
- Check spelling by proofreading, using the PowerPoint spelling checker, and have another person read the slides.
- Keep charts and graphs simple and easy to read.

Bells and Whistles

You can make your slides more interesting by adding sounds or animations. Sounds are excellent at getting the participant's attention and can be used to emphasize key points. When adding sounds to your presentation, use the .WAV format. Sound files can be found nearly everywhere on the Internet; however, be careful about copyright violations. Look for and use sound files that are not copyrighted or those that are free to use in any presentation. When including sounds in your presentation, be sure that the computer, projector, or other audiovisual equipment that you will be using can play the sounds. Many A/V systems cannot play sounds. Either ask about sound capability or test it, making changes or improvising when needed.

Animation is another way to make your presentations more interesting. Use animation to emphasize a key point or to build an idea onto another. Animation should be used sparingly, as too much animation is distracting—the audience may be waiting for the next animation rather than paying attention to the information on the slide or delivered by the speaker.

You can make your presentation seem more polished by setting up slide transitions—different ways to make a slide disappear from the screen and the next one appear. Try different transitions until you find one or two that you like. Do not change the transition for each slide.

Final Touches

After creating your slide presentation, make sure all of your slides are in the proper order. Once the sequence is correct, be sure to include an introduction and a conclusion slide. Your introductory slide states your objectives for the presentation and, if necessary, the meeting's agenda. A way to remember the intent of the introduction slide is that the introduction is where you "tell 'em what you will tell 'em."

Your conclusion slide is your summary. Summarize your entire presentation, reminding the participants of the key points. This slide should leave the participants with strong memories of your presentation. A way to remember the intent of the conclusion slide is that the conclusion is where you "tell 'em what you told 'em."

Finally, end your slide presentation with a title slide. This gives the audience the name of the presentation as they leave the room and is a reminder of the experience.

Your Final Product

Once you have developed your slides, proofread them carefully, checking for typographical and spelling errors, and put them into proper sequence, you are ready for a "reality check"—rehearsing your presentation. When getting ready to rehearse, be sure that you have notes and other materials at your disposal. Create note pages using slides at the top of the page and large print in the note section. You should be able to read your notes in low light. Once your notes and slides are ready, it is time to practice.

Contrary to the cliché that practice makes perfect, rehearsing your presentation makes it both perfect and permanent. You should practice the presentation several times—when you are sitting at your desk, at home in your living room, *and* in the meeting room prior to the actual session. When rehearsing your presentation you are not attempting to memorize it; rather, you are getting intimately familiar with the topic, so much so that the audience thinks you are talking extemporaneously. Rehearsing is not just for beginners. Subject matter experts rehearse presentations so that it provides them with confidence in the topic as well as comfort in the timing and methods of the delivery.

There are a few tips to follow when rehearsing:

- Do not read your notes, and never read your slides.
- Make eye contact with everyone in the room. Work the room from every angle.

- Be positive in your approach to speaking. Your attitude will come across to the audience very quickly.
- Know that your audience wants you to succeed, so imagine it enthusiastically applauding you.
- Make sure there is a beverage available. A warm drink helps relax the mouth and throat, whereas a cold drink, especially a carbonated beverage, can be irritating.
- Yawn. Yawning can stimulate salivation and alleviate a dry mouth.
- Stretch face and neck muscles to ease any tension.
- Take a few deep breaths, then practice your presentation.
- Be sure to talk louder than you think you need to, because, depending on the room's acoustics, your voice may not carry well.

Keep in mind that, by rehearsing, your delivery will sound less mechanical and more conversational. It also shows that you are comfortable with the material and that you respect the audience's attendance and time. No one can be perfect, but you can be prepared.

Handouts

Once you have designed your presentation, you need to develop handouts to give to the participants. Handouts are your link to the group—something that they can review in order to recall the information that you presented. While there are no hard and fast rules for developing handouts, here are some guidelines that may help you create effective handouts for your audience:

- Have enough handouts for everyone. A good rule of thumb is to print 10 percent more handouts than the number of participants registered for the program.
- Make sure that the handout relates to the information being taught.
- Limit the number of pages. People do not mind browsing through a few pages to locate the information, but if you give them too many pages, they will never look through them. If you are using PowerPoint slides, you can print your presentation in a handout format containing from one to six slides per page. Too many slides per page will shrink the slides to an unreadable size. Be sure the slides are readable.
- Leave room on the page for the participants to take notes. This feature is also available in PowerPoint when printing three slides per page. A section for notes will be placed to the right of each slide.
- Put a title on the notes. A clear title will make for easier identification when the participants look for the notes at a later date.
- If not using PowerPoint slides or the slide handout, provide an outline of the presentation.
- Use bold print or underline key points.
- Make the information easy to read by allowing for adequate spacing between lines and key points.
- Keep the information concise. Avoid jargon and unnecessary information.
- Determine when to distribute the handouts. If you want the group to take notes, distribute the handouts at the beginning of the program. If note taking is not critical, distribute the materials toward the end of the presentation.

- Unless cost is a critical factor, print on one side of the page. The rustling of pages being turned and flipped over can be distracting.

Handouts are an effective learning tool both during and after the training session. Use them, but not to excess.

SUMMARY

Teaching a class, whether it is an initial EMT or paramedic program or continuing education session, can be fun. But, to be fun, there is a lot of work that goes into preparing for the session. This chapter has given you insights into developing your presentation, especially one using slides. In creating your presentation, you need to determine a theme and then apply it to the color scheme of the slides. In addition to color, text font and the formatting of the slides are important. Once the slides have been developed, you can add graphics, animation, and sound to polish your show. But, as important as creating a good slide show is, rehearsing the show is critical. Great slides can be hampered by an unrehearsed presentation.

Slides are visual reminders of your topic. They should be clear, neat, and concise, emphasizing the points in your presentation. Designing your slides is a lot easier with the introduction of Microsoft PowerPoint. Since many participants are visual learners, a good slide program will do wonders to enhance the learning experience.

22

Scene Survey

Your Classroom Is "the Scene"

In previous chapters we talked about crafting the presentations that you will make. This chapter will delve more deeply into one of those aspects—knowing your classroom or becoming intimately familiar with the meeting place. By knowing where you will be teaching, you can avoid some of the mishaps that could occur if you were in totally unfamiliar surroundings.

When asked to speak at a seminar or conduct a class in a new environment, there are several things about knowing the room that will help make your presentation effective instead of one that is wrought with errors. Being familiar with the classroom, conference room, lecture hall, or wherever the presentation will be given does several things. It allows you to feel at ease in unfamiliar surroundings. It also gives you a sense of being welcomed by an old friend—knowing the lighting, the audiovisual capabilities, and sense of the room—all of which develop a sense of belonging, reducing the fear that something can go wrong.

Arriving at a new class or conference room is like arriving on the scene of a call. When you get dispatched to the call, you think about the nature of the call and what might be there when you arrive. As you arrive at "the scene," you scope the surroundings, looking for things such as scene safety and clues to what happened. You get a sense of the scene within a few seconds.

When arriving at a new classroom you will do a similar survey—but this time you will survey the teaching environment—learning the layout of and getting a "feel" for the room. There are several components to the "scene survey" that you need to consider, some of which can be considered far in advance of the actual presentation.

DISPATCHED

When asked to present a topic for a class, you will, most likely, be given some information about the class you will be teaching, such as the nature of the audience and location of the class. Unless you have been specifically told, ask about the number of participants expected and the type of meeting room that you will be using. For example, ask if the meeting will be held in a business office conference room, school classroom, convention center meeting room, or elementary or high school cafeteria. Also ask what type of presentation or audiovisual aids will be available. These include a screen, projector, and dry erase board or chalkboard. If slides are to be used, ask if the projector is front or rear projection. With rear projection, the projector is behind the screen and, if you are using 35mm slides, you will have to turn your slides around. This brief information can give you a sense of the meeting place even though the class is several weeks to months away.

Type of Room and Setup

The business office conference room is generally small, with limited seating. It tends to have a large conference table around which are ten to fifteen chairs. Business meeting rooms may or may not have any audiovisual aids such as projectors or screens, but you can ask for these when you determine the type of presentation to be made. A school classroom generally has desks, tables, chairs, a projection screen, and chalkboard or dry erase board. It may also have an easel and pads and other audiovisual aids. A conference center meeting room has a number of possibilities. It might be a large ballroom seating two thousand or more or a medium-sized facility that will hold fifty. All audiovisual aids usually have to be ordered in advance, so planning your presentation is critical. An elementary or high school cafeteria poses unique concerns. All audiovisual aids must be brought into the facility and set up, usually just before the presentation. These facilities also present lighting and acoustic challenges. Miniblinds or, perhaps, no blinds covering the windows can permit too much light into the room, obscuring the view of your slides. Acoustic challenges also need to be considered. Since cafeteria walls tend not to absorb sounds, your voice may "bounce" off the walls and have a harsher tone than normal. A way to overcome having to speak loudly and have your voice echo off the walls is to get your group closer to you, perhaps in a circle, where you do not have to speak as loudly or use a microphone. However, this technique will only work with a smaller number of participants. Poor acoustics can take work to overcome.

Arriving On-Scene—Arrive Early

If at all possible, get to the meeting place early. For major conferences or seminars, getting to the meeting location a day ahead is preferable. For smaller venues, this may not be possible, so arrive at least an hour or more before your class is scheduled to start. To help in your "size-up," use the following checklist. If an item is inadequate, make a note and ask, if possible, it can be changed:

Scoping the Room—A Checklist

- ☐ Conference room
- ☐ Classroom
- ☐ Theater
- ☐ Rounds or squares
- ☐ Sufficient for number of attendees
- ☐ Podium/dais
- ☐ Lectern
- ☐ Microphone
- ☐ Speakers
- ☐ Head table
- ☐ Dry erase board/chalkboard/easel with pad
- ☐ Markers/chalk
- ☐ Projector
- ☐ Screen

- □ Remote control
- □ Power source
- □ Internet connection
- □ Light switch(es)
- □ Windows/shades
- □ HVAC
- □ Background noise
- □ Acoustics

Check the Setup

When you arrive at the meeting room, note the setup. If the room has not been set up prior to your arrival, you may be the person moving the tables and chairs. There are several styles of meeting room setups, such as classroom, theater, conference room, and table rounds or squares, to name a few. In a classroom style, there are tables and chairs facing the dais or podium, lending itself more to a lecture format presentation. People attending the meeting can place items such as notebooks or refreshments on the table to use throughout the session. A classroom-style setup may also consist of individual desks like those found in school classrooms.

In theater-style seating, the chairs are neatly placed in rows, but there are no tables the participants can use to take notes. This setting involves listening to a prepared presentation with minimal or no activities or note taking planned.

A conference style generally consists of a large table or several smaller tables pushed together in the center of the room. Chairs are positioned around the table, and participants can address each other as well as the speaker. Conference-style seating is preferred when the attendees will be working together on assigned projects.

With block-style seating, round tables or rectangular tables pushed together into squares are positioned around the room, creating seating for students in several small groups. This style can be used for work groups or small group assignments.

In all instances, be sure that there are more than enough chairs for the anticipated number of participants. A good overage is 10 percent of registered participants. If there are too many tables and chairs in the room, you may want to remove some to bring the group closer together or more toward the front of the meeting room.

Dais, Lectern, Podium

After noting the seating arrangement, take a look at where you will be speaking. Before getting into specifics, there are a few terms that need clarification. A dais refers to a raised platform. A dais can be large and allow a speaker to move around and address segments of the audience. In contrast, a podium is a small, raised platform on which a speaker stands. It might be easier to think of a podium as the raised platform on which a conductor stands when leading an orchestra. A lectern, according to *Webster's Dictionary,* is "a stand used to support a book in a convenient position for a standing reader." Thus, you may be on a dais or podium and may or may not have a lectern on which to place your notes.

If a dais, lectern, or podium is present, note its position relative to the audience, projector, and screen. If no dais, lectern, or podium is provided, you will be standing on the floor at the same level as the participants. Some of whom, especially those in the back of the room, may not be able to see you.

Stand on the dais or podium and look out over the empty chairs, noting if each chair is visible from where you are standing. If all the chairs cannot be seen, it might be necessary to move from a fixed location to let everyone see you. If the lectern is on a dais, note the dais's size and whether you will be able to move around to address sections of the audience. Note the limitations of the dais and where it ends. It is very embarrassing to fall off the dais in the middle of a dynamic presentation. Also note how to get onto and off of the dais. If there are steps, be sure to use them. If no steps are available, note the height of the dais that you will have to climb onto to deliver your presentation.

If you will have a beverage while speaking—something that is highly recommended to overcome dry mouth—be sure there is a place to put the drink. The top of the lectern is slanted and not a good place to put any liquid-filled glass unless you want to risk spilling it on yourself, your notes, or your computer. A lectern may have a lower shelf for storage. Use the lower shelf to place any beverage or other necessary items. If no shelf is available, use a head table or other suitable flat surface.

Place your notes on the lectern and make sure that you can see them. A light on the lectern should be bright enough for you to review your notes when necessary without distracting the audience.

Audiovisuals

If you will be using audiovisual equipment such as a slide projector, locate the remote control. If you will be using your laptop computer, note the location of the projector and the cable to connect between your computer and the projector. Equally important, note the location of electrical power. If necessary, bring or ask for an extension cord.

Be sure to know how you will advance your slides. If you are using a slide projector, a remote can be used from the lectern, but you might have to stick close to the lectern when delivering your presentation. There is a way around being stuck in one place. You can use a radio-activated or an infrared remote. These wireless devices will allow you to move around and away from the lectern and projector to directly address the participants sitting in the corners of the room. The range of these devices can vary, so be sure to determine the range before your presentation starts.

If you will be using a laptop computer and multimedia projector, the same concept applies—know how you will advance your slides. When using PowerPoint or Keynote, you can advance your slides by clicking on the mouse, hitting the "Return" key, or using the arrow keys. But this limits your movement from the lectern. An optical mouse is one option, but that will allow you only five to six feet of space between you and the computer. A radio-activated mouse made by Logitech (Trackman Live) or Keyspan are potential solutions. These devices allow you to be thirty to forty feet away from the computer. Again, determine the total range of the device inside the meeting room before you start your presentation. If you are using any remote control device, be sure to have extra batteries on hand to change when the old ones fail. As a precaution, you might want to put in fresh batteries before your presentation starts.

Determine if the meeting room uses front projection or rear projection. Front projection means that the projector is in front of the screen. If so, your 35mm slides are ready to show. Rear projection means that the projector is behind the screen. If you are using 33mm slides, you will have to turn your slides around so they can be read. Otherwise, the text will be backward. If you are using a laptop computer and multimedia projector in a rear-projection format, reverse the slides using the menu option for the projector.

If you will be using an easel and pads or overhead transparencies, make sure that the group will be able to see the easel and pad or overhead. Write something on the pad or turn on the overhead projector using one of your transparencies, then walk around the room. Go to each corner of the room as well as the back. Make sure that people sitting in those seats will be able to see the easel and pad or overhead transparency.

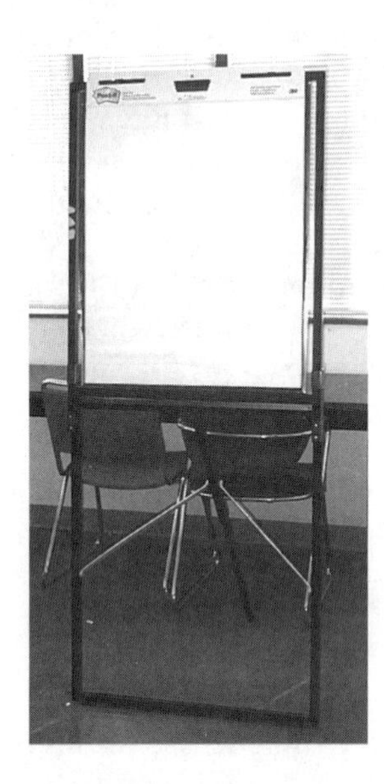

If the meeting room is small and you tend to project your voice, you may not need a microphone. In contrast, if the room and group are large or your voice does not project in a large room, you may need to use a microphone. Locate the microphone and test it. Also locate the volume and sensitivity control box. If there is a fixed and corded microphone attached to the lectern, it will restrict your movements and limit your actions to the immediate area of the lectern.

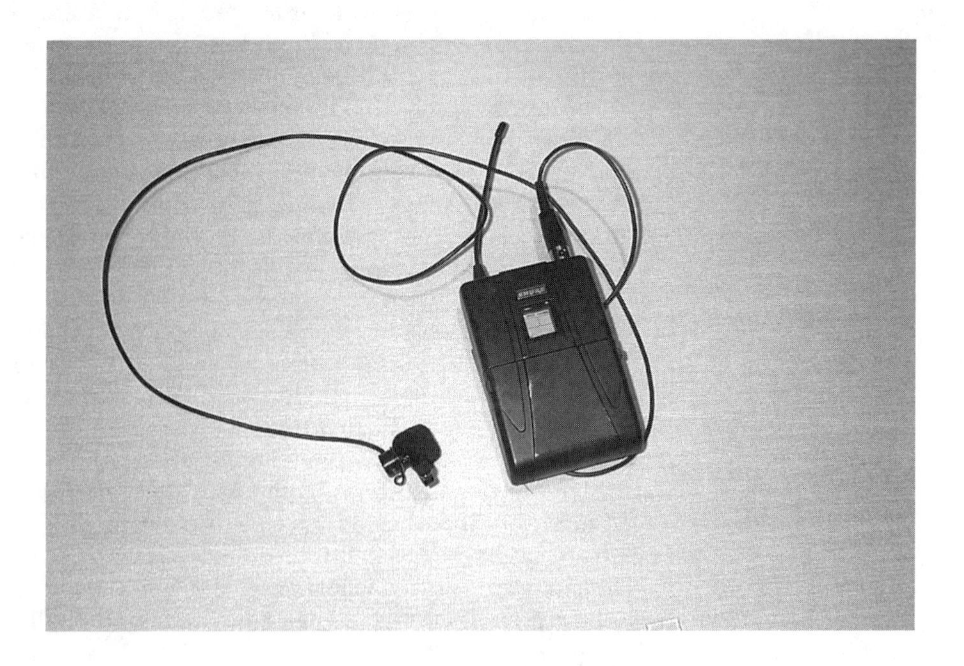

Turn the microphone on and test it. Note the speaker system in the room. If your voice is too loud, you might need to turn the volume down or back away from the microphone. Also note any feedback—that squealing sound that seems to injure eardrums. If there is feedback, try changing the position of the microphone or holding it further away from your mouth. Also, move away from any speakers. Standing underneath or next to a speaker quickly causes feedback. If necessary, turn the microphone sensitivity down.

If possible, use a lavaliere microphone—a microphone that clips onto your tie or shirt with a transmitter that attaches to your belt. As with remote-control clickers, be sure to have an extra battery around just in case the one in the microphone fails.

HVAC (Heating, Ventilation, Air Conditioning)

Many people have complained about the temperature inside a meeting room, saying it is too cold. A room is typically set colder than normal for a reason—once you get all the bodies inside, the room will warm up quickly. If the room is warm before the participants arrive, cooling the room after it is full and too warm can be difficult. In addition, keeping a room slightly cool tends to keep the audience awake.

When you first arrive at the meeting room to scope it out, get a sense of the heating and cooling possibilities. If the room is too warm or cold, look for the thermostat or ask maintenance to adjust the temperature. Be careful what you ask for, since correcting an error can be very difficult in some meeting facilities.

Lighting

Locate the light switches and make sure you know how they work and which lights they control. Note any dimmers and change the setting to what is desired for your presentation. In some facilities, you can preset the lighting and, with the flip of a switch, the lighting will immediately change to your settings. This is more of a rarity than a reality. So, know how to increase or decrease the lighting in your room. If you are in a large room, you may need a colleague to set the lights once your presentation starts and adjust them as needed.

Turn on the projector and look at a slide and how the light affects viewing it. If there is a glare on the screen from any light, make every attempt to change it. Turn off the light, or, if necessary, remove the bulb, especially if you cannot move the projector or screen.

Get a Feel for the Room

Before any of the participants arrive, sit in the back of the meeting room and spend a few minutes of quiet time to absorb the sense of the room—getting to know its personality. When all is quiet, like during the still of the night, you can perceive the room and some of its idiosyncrasies. Look at the floor, walls, and ceiling and "feel" the room. We are not talking about anything metaphysical or paranormal. Rather, each meeting room has its own "nature." While you are probably not the first to speak in the room and will not be the last, there is some history in the room created by those who went before you. After a while, especially after practicing listening to the room, you will get a sense of its friendliness or warmth—a sense of its "personality." If the room seems cold and distant to you, it will feel that way to the participants in your class, creating an environment that is resistant to learning. It will be up to you to make the room warm and inviting. To change the nature of a cold room, be prepared to smile a lot and personally greet most, if not all, of the participants.

Rehearse

Once you have scoped out the room and become familiar with your surroundings, rehearse your presentation. Go through your slides once, twice, or three or more times to review your presentation. While you are rehearsing, move around the room. Go from the front to the back, and to each corner. Look at your presentation as your participants will and make sure that your slides are viewable and readable. Do a last-minute check for errors such as typos or misspelled words. Remember, there is no such thing as "winging it."

PLAN B (OR C, D, E . . .)

Always have a Plan B or other contingency plans in the event that something just does not work right. Not only must you have a Plan B, you must always be prepared to use it. Projector bulbs burn out, remote control device batteries fail, sound systems squeal, computer files become corrupt.

The projector bulb just blew!

Whenever possible, have backup projector bulbs available. Not only should a spare bulb be available, it should also be one that works in your projector. Projector bulbs will burn out, and they take a few minutes to change, prolonging your presentation. But most audiences accept minor inconveniences and do not blame the instructor for a bulb burning out. Be careful when changing bulbs— the one that just burned out may be very hot.

The remote control doesn't work!

As mentioned earlier, remote control devices have batteries that will eventually fail. Spare batteries are easily replaced with a minimum of delay in your presentation.

The audience is covering its ears from the microphone feedback!

A poor sound system can make even the most melodious voice sound hideous. If you are using a convention center meeting room, audiovisual staff is usually on-hand and can quickly respond to a call for help. If no one is available to assist you, be prepared to make some minor adjustments in the control settings.

The computer screen flashes "Warning, Battery Low," then dies!

Computers are great tools, but like anything else, they, too, can fail. Hard drives crash, files become corrupt, batteries die, and operating systems fail. Be sure to have a backup copy of your presentation immediately available. Depending on the size of your presentation and computer configuration, you might need a floppy disk, Zip disk, or CD.

Do not rely upon battery power to deliver your entire presentation. Take and use your power supply, using battery power only in an emergency. In a worst-case scenario, your computer may fail. Operating systems can become corrupt and fail to boot your computer. It might be necessary to borrow a computer and use the backup disk or install your slides onto the other machine. You may also have to quickly print your slides to film and have them produced in a 33mm format. Again, having a backup plan and being prepared to implement it is essential.

SUMMARY

After spending hours developing objectives, lesson plans, and a dynamic slide presentation, it is equally important to get to know where your presentation will be held. There are a number of meeting rooms that can hold your session, each with its own, unique features. It is very important for you to know your meeting room and all of the features as well as the idiosyncrasies. Arriving at the location well in advance and scoping the place can forestall disasters. Knowing the room, its setup, audiovisuals, lighting, and HVAC will help make your presentation one that has tremendous favorable impact on the participants. After all, the slide presentation as well as the meeting room and all of its accoutrements are extensions of you.

23

Presentation Excellence

Show Them What It's All About

In Chapter 22, we talked about designing your presentation, including using slides to highlight the information. We also talked about the importance of rehearsing the presentation to become intimately familiar with it so that you sound confident and credible. Finally, Chapter 22 gave you some tips for rehearshing and presenting your topic. But the challenge, of course, is giving the actual presentation—getting in front of a group and delivering your topic.

Every person has a unique delivery style that develops over time. But when starting out as a field training officer with minimal teaching experience, your style is raw and undeveloped. Most dynamic speakers refined their presentation skills over time, but they all started out at the same place—untrained in public speaking and not knowing where to begin. The purpose of this chapter is to give you some thoughts about your actual presentation—from where to stand to timing and techniques to handling questions.

AT THE STARTING GATE

On the day of the presentation, especially if it is one of your first teaching assignments, you need to scope out the meeting room and do one last rehearsal (see Chapter 22). Make sure you know where everything is and are mentally prepared to do a great job. Here are a few tips for gearing up and starting out on the day of the presentation:

- Walk off the jitters. If you are nervous, walk around the room to alleviate nervous energy *before* anyone arrives.
- If someone will introduce you, be sure to smile during the introduction and, immediately afterward, shake their hand and openly thank them.
- Just as you are about to begin, as the audience is quieting, smile at the participants, take a subtle deep breath, and relax.
- As you did when you rehearsed, be preparted to talk louder than you think you need.
- Remember the five Cs of presenting:
  - Confident
  - Credible
  - Competent

    - Convincing
    - Comfortable
- Most important, have fun!

TAKE A STAND

If possible, stand on the left side of the room (from the audience's view) at an approximate fourty-five-degree angle to the audience. There are a few reasons for this approach. First, it is nonthreatening to the audience, allowing an open position from which you can gesture or move. Second, the audience's gaze can easily shift to the right to look at your slides and back to look at you. Finally, you are less likely to stand in front of the screen and block the view of the slide.

Be careful not to stand in front of a light. The audience's eyes will be attracted more to the light than to you.

Opening

Even if you have been introduced by another person, smile and reintroduce yourself. If you are beginning without an introduction, be sure to introduce yourself, especially if you are talking in front of an unfamiliar group. Begin with a story or a humorous anecdote. If you are telling a joke, be safe—be politically correct. Self-deprecating humor (a story about yourself) usually works well and helps establish rapport with the audience. Finally, depending on the group and the setting of the presentation, you may want to use an "ice breaker" to get everyone more comfortable.

There are several ice breakers that have been successfully used to begin a presentation. Some feel that telling a quick joke or two is a good way to begin, although most agree that the day of the one-liner has passed. Other speakers have developed techniques that invite participation in the session. This chapter will discuss various ice breakers that you can use. By using an effective ice breaker, your group will be more relaxed and receptive to the information you are sharing.

Please note, this is not an all-inclusive discussion of ice breakers, nor will all of the ice breakers work in all situations. Since each group is unique, any ice breaker you use needs to be tailored to the specific group and situation.

Who Are You and What Do You Want?

This ice breaker acts to introduce each participant to the entire group. Have each one stand up and introduce him or herself, stating information about who he or she is, where he or she works, and a personal interest. Information from the participants might include:

- Name
- City where they live
- Employer
- What they like most about their job
- Hobbies
- Place they would like to go
- Something that not many people know about them
- Someone, living or dead, that they would like to have dinner with

A variation on this theme is "Who Are They, What Do They Want?" In this variation, have the participants pair off and interview each other. If possible, pair people who do not know each other well or at all. Also, have the participant state expectations about the program. After the participants have interviewed each other for about twenty minutes, have them introduce each other to the group.

Toilet Paper

Take a roll of toilet paper into the room and pass it around to each participant. Have each participant tear off as much as they need without telling them any reason for the toilet paper. After everyone has taken some toilet paper, have the participants tear it along the perforations and count the total number of sheets in their cache. For each square of toilet paper, the participant must state an interesting facet about himself or herself.

Draw a Pig

This was developed by Gordon Cotton of New Brunswick, Canada. If you will be providing some intense information about managing or motivating employees or students, you might want to begin your presentation by having everyone draw a pig. In this activity, participants are asked to draw a pig using a blank sheet of paper (their own, or you may provide a sheet). If anyone asks what the pig should look like, tell that person that the pig is unique to you and that no other instructions are necessary. After ten minutes, have the group put down their pens or pencils so that you can provide the results of the exercise. Make sure each person scores his or her own pig.

The results are based on several characteristics.

Where on the paper is the pig drawn?

- If the pig is drawn on the top of the page, you are positive and optimistic.
- If the pig is drawn in the middle of the page, you are a realist.
- If the pig is drawn on the bottom of the page, you are pessimistic and may behave negatively.

Which way is the pig facing?

- If the pig is facing left, you believe in tradition, are friendly, and remember dates.
- If the pig is facing right, you are innovative and active, but have no sense of family and do not remember dates.
- If the pig is facing forward, you are direct, enjoy playing devil's advocate, and are not afraid of joining a discussion.

How detailed is your pig?

- A detailed pig means you are analytical, cautious, and distrustful.
- Few details means you are emotional, naive, care little for detail, and take risks.

How many legs are showing?

- If four legs are showing, you are secure, stubborn, and stick to your ideals.
- If less then four legs showing, you are insecure or experiencing a change in your life.

What about the ears?

- The bigger the ears on the pig, the better you are at listening.

What does the tail mean?

- The bigger the tail, the happier you are with your love life.

Magic Wand

Using a magic wand prop, tell everyone in the group that you have found a magic wand that will grant them three changes at work. Ask what they would change and have them give the reasons why they would change it. A slight twist on this concept involves asking what they would change if they became a supervisor or manager.

Liar, Liar

Hand out index cards to each participant and have them write four things about themselves, some of which may be outlandish, with one of those things a lie. In turn, have each participant read aloud the four things on the card and have the other participants guess which one is false.

Who Did That?

If you are familiar with the participants or are working with a close-knit group, prior to the meeting have each person submit something they did that makes them proud. For example, someone might have published an article, whereas someone else bought a house. Before the meeting, type a list of these accomplishments with a space next to each for the answer.

At the meeting, pass out the list and allow the group thirty minutes to circulate through the room interviewing the other participants to learn who did what. The participants are to write the person's name on the line next to the event. To make things more interesting, you could impose a rule that prohibits asking specifically about the event. People would be allowed to ask, "Do you like to write?" but would not be allowed to ask, "Did you write an article?"

Castaway

Divide the group into teams with an equal number of participants (if possible). Tell the teams that they have been marooned on a deserted island. On a sheet of paper, they are to write five items they would have brought with them. Note that the five items are for the entire team, not for each person.

After fifteen minutes have each team list the items they would have brought and compare the list with other teams. Allow others to question the items brought to the deserted island.

Main Event

Once you have delivered the opener, present a short description or headline of the presentation. The headliner should contain key points that you want the audience to retain. After the headliner, present the heart of the topic and, at the end, close by summarizing the entire presentation in a few short sentences. If you can, save the best for last, since you want the audience to remember you and the topic with strong, positive memories. There is a phrase that highlights this concept: The audience may not remember what you said or how you said it, but they will remember forever how you made them feel.

Let the group walk away with strong, positive feelings and you have done a good job.

Some Tips for Talking to the Group

Maintain good eye contact. Look at the group, find a person, and look at them. Stay with them for a few moments and make a connection before moving to the next person. Work the whole room and never turn your back on them. If you have to move to the back of the dais, toward the screen or to the lectern, walk backward.

Vary your voice. While you are speaking to the audience, as in a conversation, you need to speak louder than normal. Note that as you increase volume, you increase inflection. If you want to draw your audience in, speak a little quieter. You may even notice that the members lean forward to pay closer attention. Also vary your pitch. It makes you sound enthusiastic and keeps the group's attention.

Pause after key points. Speak a key point or phase and pause for a moment, then speak another key point. But beware of too many pauses. You do not want to sound choppy, like some politicians when they speak three or four words and then pause only to finish the sentence in the next three or four words. Speaking in such a fashion can be distracting, if not annoying.

Do not read your presentation and, if using slides, never read your slides. You should be so comfortable with the presenation that you do not need many, if any, notes. If you are using notes, they should contain key comments that you want to cover. These should serve as memory joggers.

Be enthusiastic. Enjoy and have fun with your topic, sharing that enjoyment and passion with the audience. Enthusiasm is infectious, but you have to give it to the audience in order to get it back.

Body language is important. Use hand and arm movements to emphasize a point. Avoid crossing your arms and do not point at the group. A friendly gesture such as an extended palm will bring a group to you rather than push it away. If you clasp your hands, keep them clasped for only a few moments. If they remain clasped for more than ten seconds, the group will begin to look at your hands and not at you.

Timing is important. Be aware of your time limits. Most lecterns have clocks. If one is not avalailable on the lectern, perhaps there is a clock on the wall in the room. Glance at it occasionally, but never deliberately look at your watch. If there is no clock in the room or on the lectern, you can discreetly look at your watch when making an arm or hand gesture. But timing is more than keeping within the time limits—it also means synchronizing your presentation. You may also want to think of it as choreographing your presentation. Below are some thoughts to help you choreograph your talk:

- When moving from one side of the room to the other, be in midsentence. This adds continuity and shows finesse.
- Wait to sip your drink until there is an appropriate pause, such as laughter at an anecdote, or applause during a key point.
- For a unique or extremely important point, pause for three to four seconds to achieve complete silence before stating your key point.

Hit emotional buttons. Get to the heart of the audience and trigger their emotions. Hitting those emotional buttons will ensure more impact.

Remember that stage fright is merely a negative term for excitement. Even the most seasoned speakers are nervous immediately before their presentation begins. If you are excessively nervous, walk around, making an effort to turn your nervousness into enthusiasm.

The Q-and-A Period

Many presentations will end with a question-and-answer session. You can use this time to stimulate the audience's thoughts, begin conversation with the group, and improve its retention of the information. If you will be allowing time for a question-and-answer session, prepare in advance for the types of questions you may get.

When opening up the session to questions and answers, remember that most people do not want to appear foolish in front of their peers; thus, they will avoid asking about something they do not understand. To break the ice, have a few questions prepared to ask them and, if necessary, ask yourself.

When someone asks a question, be sure to answer it effectively. Below are some tips for the Q-and-A session. If you ask the group a question:

- Avoid questions that can be answered yes or no.
- Ask general questions initially.
- Ask specific questions on one topic at a time.
- When someone is answering your question, do not interrupt.

If your group is asking a question:

- Listen to the entire question. Do not assume what the person is asking and jump in prematurely.
- Repeat the question so that everyone in the room can hear it. If necessary, ask the person what is meant by the question or to clarify it.

- Answer the question and verify whether your answer satisfies the person.
- Avoid being negative or unresponsive. Also avoid diverting from the question or going on a tangential discussion.
- If you are not familiar with the answer, say so, but tell the group that you will get the information and let them know as soon as possible. If the participants are unfamiliar to you, ask for a contact person or an e-mail address for those interested in the answer. The e-mail address can be obtained after the session has ended.

After the Session

As your presentation ends, thank everyone for their attendance and wish them well. As the participants leave, there may be a few stragglers who have additional questions. Answer those questions appropriately.

Once the participants have left, debrief the session. Meet with someone you trust who was in the audience and ask for their critique. If you presented the topic with others, debrief with them at a convenient time so that they can share their thoughts on the entire session.

Be sure to research information from the question-and-answer session that you were unable to answer at the time. Send the information to the group in a timely manner.

Take a deep breath. You are finished—for now!

24

Effectiveness of Training

Critiquing the Program

After the training session has been completed, we often wonder how effective it was and if the participants actually learned something. Frequently, we hand out evaluation forms for the participants' use to critique what they heard and saw. But that type of evaluation is only a part of the critique process. This chapter will discuss training program evaluation and how the field training officer can use these tools to improve overall training.

There are many times when a training session can be evaluated and many ways to do it. Ideally, the program should be assessed throughout its development (formative evaluation) as well as after the program has been delivered (summary evaluation). Initially, the person requesting the program (manager, supervisor, or commander) should evaluate the session before it is conducted to ensure it is what is needed and wanted. Second, the program should be evaluated by peers to ensure the adequacy and accuracy of the program's design prior to and immediately after it is presented. The reason for the ongoing evaluation is to provide feedback to ensure that the training is linked to the work that the participants perform, especially from a quality assurance perspective. If there is no link between the training and the actual work, can the cost of the training be justified?

An assessment of the training will also provide information about the program and its ability to be transferred to the job. Questions concerning behavioral change on the job can be answered by an evaluation of the program and its relationship to job performance. For example, if an employee is referred to training because of poor performance in a specific area, did the employee's performance significantly improve as a result of the intervention?

Most EMS agencies are probably conducting some form of training program evaluation. But these evaluations are superficial at best. Most field training officers are not fully aware of what makes up training evaluation since they have not been trained in evaluation methodology. In addition, evaluation of training takes time, personnel, and money, which is limited in EMS agencies.

Before assessing a program, the field training officer should determine if the evaluation would be cost effective. Also, the field training officer needs to know what training should be evaluated and to what extent.

Before developing and beginning a training session evaluation, the field training officer should quickly determine whether:

- The training had an impact on the EMS agency
- The trainees are using the new information or skills on the job
- The trainees have demonstrated new knowledge, skills, and attitudes on the job
- The investment in time and money was worth the return.

KIRKPATRICK'S TECHNIQUES

In late 1959 and early 1960, Donald Kirkpatrick wrote a series of articles in the *Journal for the American Society for Training Directors* entitled "Techniques for Evaluating Training Programs." In these articles and works that followed, Kirkpatrick developed his model of four levels that sequentially build upon each other. In essence, each higher level is a more precise evaluation of the training program. Unfortunately, each successive level requires more time and energy. The levels that Kirkpatrick identified include: Reaction, Learning, Transfer, and Results. A fifth level, Return on Investment, was developed later and is beyond the scope of the field training officer.

Level 1 Evaluation—Reaction

Level 1 Evaluation, or Reaction, is simply described as how well the participants liked the session. For this reason, it is often called a "Smiley" evaluation. It is conducted at the end of the program by handing out an evaluation form, asking the participants for their feedback. The next page contains a sample "Smiley" evaluation.

As is evident, the Level 1 Evaluation does not assess whether learning occurred. It is merely a reflection of the participant's impression of the program. While a favorable Level 1 Evaluation should invite pride in a job well done, it should also be viewed humbly since, again, learning is not indicated, nor is a transfer to on-the-job-performance shown. In reviewing the "Smiley" evaluations, the best place to look for candid assessments is in the written comments. Many participants check the Strongly Agree or Agree box without taking the time to thoroughly evaluate the program. To determine if learning took place during the session, it is necessary to step up to a Level 2 Evaluation.

Level 2 Evaluation—Learning

In this level of evaluation, learning is limited to what information was understood and absorbed by the participants. It does not relate to on-the-job performance. There are two ways to assess learning. The first method is to administer a pretest and a posttest. The second method is to administer an embedded test.

A pretest and posttest is a simple way to measure learning. Each test should be identical so that learning can be related to the program. The participants can take the pretest at the start of the session or at their leisure, prior to attending the program. The posttest can be given to the participants at the conclusion of the session and the results compared quickly. Questions should be based on key points in the program as well as on information the participants may have already had in prior sessions.

The tests need to be constructed objectively, such as multiple choice, true–false, and matching, to avoid subjective interpretation of the answers. Once the tests have been scored and recorded, the results should be given to the participants as soon as possible. When possible, a data analysis should be performed on each question as well as on the entire test to determine validity and establish confidence in the test.

Please take a moment to complete this evaluation. It will help us to continue to develop and provide quality training for you. Your feedback is important to us. Thank you!

Date: ___ / ___ / 2003 **Program Name:** ______________________________
Location of Training: ______________________________
Name: ______________________________ (voluntary)
Instructor: ______________________________ **Guest Speaker:** ______________________________

1. **What is your overall level of satisfaction with the program?**
   ☐ Excellent ☐ Very Good ☐ Good ☐ Fair ☐ Poor
2. **Comments to explain Fair or Poor rating.**

____

____

3. **The program prepared me to:**

	Strongly Agree	Agree	Neutral	Disagree	Strongly Disagree
(Insert course objectives here.)	☐	☐	☐	☐	☐
	☐	☐	☐	☐	☐
	☐	☐	☐	☐	☐
	☐	☐	☐	☐	☐

4. **Comments to explain any Disagree or Strongly Disagree rating.**

____

____

5. **The instructor:**

	Strongly Agree	Agree	Neutral	Disagree	Strongly Disagree
Was organized and kept the program on track	☐	☐	☐	☐	☐
Encouraged interaction and participation	☐	☐	☐	☐	☐
Encouraged and addressed questions appropriately	☐	☐	☐	☐	☐
Was credible and knowledgeable on the topics	☐	☐	☐	☐	☐
Promoted a positive learning environment	☐	☐	☐	☐	☐

6. **Please rate the effectiveness of the guest speaker's presentation (if applicable).**

	Strongly Agree	Agree	Neutral	Disagree	Strongly Disagree
The guest speaker was informative and knowledgeable on the topics presented.	☐	☐	☐	☐	☐
The information presented will be useful to me when I return to my job.	☐	☐	☐	☐	☐

7. **Please explain any Disagree or Strongly Disagree ratings of instructor or guest speaker.**

____

____

8. **The program:**

	Strongly Agree	Agree	Neutral	Disagree	Strongly Disagree
Was well planned and organized	☐	☐	☐	☐	☐
Included adequate and realistic examples and/or applications	☐	☐	☐	☐	☐
Provided materials (handouts, etc.) that were helpful	☐	☐	☐	☐	☐
Prepared me to use the information when I return to my job	☐	☐	☐	☐	☐

9. **To improve the program, I would:**

____

____

____

____

____

10. **Recommendations for future programs:**

____

____

____

Thank you!

An embedded test is one that the instructor gives during the session. Call it a pop quiz or any other name; the embedded test can be verbal or written. Since there is no pretest to assess entry-level knowledge, it will be difficult to determine whether the answers were generated from the session or from another source. Further, if the embedded test is given verbally, not everyone will have the opportunity to answer. Thus, individual learning will not be fully determined.

Level 3 Evaluation—Transfer (Behavior)

This level evaluation is more difficult than the previous two because it has to account for many factors that lead to behavioral change. Initially, a systematic on-the-job performance appraisal must be conducted before and after the training has been conducted. The "before" test will establish a baseline performance from which future assessments can be compared.

The performance assessments must be conducted as objectively as possible by several individuals—field training officer, shift supervisor, shift commander, and so forth. The more appraisals, the better the assessment and comparison. The posttraining assessment can be conducted shortly after the session as well as three months postsession to determine retention of the training. Additional assessments may be performed to help validate the study. See the next page for a sample Level 3 Evaluation.

There are several obstructions to a transfer of learning that could make such an assessment difficult to obtain. Some of the barriers include:

- Leadership of the organization does not support the training or model the behavior
- Staffing patterns make it difficult to use the knowledge and skills, or there is such a high turnover rate that the behavior does not transfer correctly or efficiently
- Compensation or pay scale is considered inadequate and stifles the will or desire to achieve
- Job description does not include use of the knowledge and skills.

These impediments do not preclude assessing the transfer of information; however, the field training officer should not be disappointed by the lack of transfer if these and other barriers are present.

Sample Level 3 Evaluation

Skill Assessment

Employee Name ______________________________ **Time on Job** ________________

Shift Supervisor' Name ________________________ **Date of Evaluation** ___________

Instructions: This evaluation is to be completed by the shift supervisor or shift commander at one month and three months after the training session has been completed. Your responses are critical to the employee's professional development as well as ongoing quality improvement of the training department. We need your partnership in assessing the transfer of knowledge and skills to on-the-job performance. Please circle the response to the questions below that best expresses your opinion. It is important to answer all items. Return the survey to training. **Thank you!**

Skill or Behavior	**Employee Began Using**	**Percent of Time Performs Skill Correctly**	**Assistance Required to Apply Skill to Job**	**Employee Has Not Applied What Was Learned Because**
Skill 1	Within 1 week	100%		Did not have opportunity to use skill
(*List each skill separately as a general skill*)	Within 1 month	75%	Coaching from partner	Did not learn what was needed to apply skill
	After more than 1 month	50%	Self-initiative	Too much time between training and opportunity
	Used skill before training	25%	Other ___________	Employee has not had time to use skill
		0%		Applying skill was deemed too risky
				Tools, supplies were not available
				Support for employee's efforts was not available

Skill or Behavior	**Employee Began Using**	**Percent of Time Performs Skill Correctly**	**Assistance Required to Apply Skill to Job**	**Employee Has Not Applied What Was Learned Because**
Skill 2	Within 1 week	100%		Did not have opportunity to use skill
(*List each skill separately as a general skill*)	Within 1 month	75%	Coaching from partner	Did not learn what was needed to apply skill
	After more than 1 month	50%	Self-initiative	Too much time between training and opportunity
	Used skill before training	25%	Other ___________	Employee has not had time to use skill
		0%		Applying skill was deemed too risky
				Tools, supplies were not available
				Support for employee's efforts was not available

The employee needed help from others to begin applying the skill to the job (circle one).

Strongly Agree Agree Neutral Disagree Strongly Disagree

What do you believe needs to be added to the training to make it more applicable to the job?

____

State any actions that need to be taken in order to improve performance in any area of development.

Level 4 Evaluation—Results

The highest level of evaluation is the most difficult and time-consuming of the four levels. Results are described as the ability to apply the knowledge and skills learned to new and unfamiliar situations. A key question to be addressed is, What value did the training bring to the organization? When conducting a Level 4 Evaluation, areas of critical impact such as turnover rate, productivity, organizational finances, morale, and teamwork are assessed. This level of assessment is most often performed by senior managers, commanders, and chiefs.

As can be seen, the higher the level of evaluation, the more it will consume time and resources. We tend to focus on Level 1 Evaluations; however, this level gives us very little information regarding the effectiveness of the training program.

SUMMARY

This chapter has focused on assessing the effectiveness of a training program. As is evident, the four levels of evaluation increase time and costs, but have much higher values in assessing the program. While a Level 1, "Smiley" evaluation will tell the field training officer that the program was enjoyable, it will not indicate whether anything was learned. A Level 2 Evaluation indicates that learning has taken place, whereas a Level 3 Evaluation shows that the learning has transferred to the job. The highest-level evaluation, Level 4, examines the impact the training had on the EMS agency. It is costly and time-consuming to conduct. Thus, the field training officer should be more focused on the first three levels of training program evaluation.

25

Making Sense Out of Dollars

Developing a Training Budget

There is a lot that goes into training and being an effective field training officer. You have to know something about human behavior and how to motivate employees, must be able to effectively communicate, need to understand some of the basics of management, have a grasp of learning theories, and be able to design an effective training program. But all of this is not free, nor is it inexpensive. An effective training program does require spending money. The FTO, especially if part of the management team, must be able to develop a budget. Senior management may ask the FTO how much money is needed to provide a training program for the employees. The purpose of this chapter is to discuss the components of a budget and demonstrate how to prepare a training budget for senior management.

When asked, "How much will training cost?" the FTO should not guess. Rather, the FTO should have a good sense of the money needed to run a training section or division. Take a look at the Sample Budget Worksheet in the Appendix. The worksheet in the Appendix has been left blank so that it may be copied for budget development. If your agency has a budget worksheet, be sure to use that form.

As you can see, there are several components that go into developing a training budget, including salaries, office expenses, travel, equipment, and more. Over the next several pages, we will detail how to determine what goes into each category.

SAMPLE BUDGET WORKSHEET EXPLAINED

Each general category, along with its components, will be explained. You will notice that many budget items have a line for justification. This provides space for you to detail how you arrived at the amount included in the budget. For example, under wages and salaries, if you merely state $100,000, you may be asked how you calculated that amount. If you include a justification such as "two field training officers at $40,000 and one office assistant at $20,000," there is a reduced chance of being questioned about the total.

Personnel expenses are the costs associated with wages and salaries paid to employees. These costs include base pay along with overtime, taxes, and Worker's Compensation. Personnel expenses also need to consider any cost-of-living adjustment (COLA) to include adjustments for inflation. This is an important component if the budget will overlap the agency's fiscal year or is a revised budget for subsequent years. Finally, personnel expenses include the costs of any employer paid benefits, such as health and dental insurance, life insurance, and a retirement or pension plan. What must be deducted from personnel expenses are those portions paid by the employee through payroll deductions.

Office expenses are all costs associated with maintaining office space if such space is needed. Included in this category are rent, utilities, printing and duplicating, postage and shipping, office supplies, and office equipment.

Travel and entertainment are costs involved in business-related travel. For example, if there are state or regional EMS meetings that you attend, the cost of travel to those meetings is included. Further, if you will be staying overnight, lodging and meals need to be included in this category. Finally, any out-of-town guest speakers or consultants who will be used in training programs will incur expense involved with travel, including airfare, lodging, meals, and miscellaneous expenses.

Dues and subscriptions are costs associated with memberships in any professional organization. It also includes subcriptions to trade journals as well as any textbooks purchased for use in training. Books such as EMT and paramedic course materials, dictionaries, and other reference works can become part of a training library.

Education and training are costs associated with attending professional conferences and seminars. Travel to the seminars is included in this category and not in "Travel and Entertainment," since the travel is for educational purposes. Associated expenses, including lodging, meals, and conference fees, are also included in this category.

Equipment costs are those associated with purchasing and maintaining training equipment as well as vehicles used by training staff. In addition to major equipment, soft goods such as disposable items need to be included. For example, if you are using bandages and splints for a training exercise, these items need to be purchased from this section of the budget. Finally, repairs and maintenance for major items are included in this section.

Personnel Expenses .... $__________

This is the sum of all of the components below, including wages and salaries, overtime, COLA, payroll taxes, and benefits

Wages and salaries .... $__________

Justification: Detailed explanation of amount on line

This is the sum of all base pay plus overtime and COLA. You can separate by individual, but a total is what is needed.

Overtime .... $__________

Justification: Detailed explanation of amount on line

If overtime is considered, approximate the amount of overtime pay. Often, it is a percent of base pay. For example, overtime costs may be close to 10 percent of base pay. Add this amount to wages and salaries above.

COLA .... $__________

Justification: Detailed explanation of amount on line

Cost of living adjustment is the percent by which salaries are increased to cover inflation and other costs of living. COLA varies each year, but has been in the range of 2 to 3 percent of all wages and salaries. Multiply the total of all wages and salaries (including overtime) by the COLA rate.

Payroll taxes .... $__________

This is the total amount the employer pays for federal and state taxes as well as Worker's Compensation, as determined below.

FICA .... __________

FICA is the Social Security contribution. The employer and employee both contribute. Currently, the FICA contribution is 6.2 percent of all wages and salaries, including overtime.

Medicare .... __________

Medicare contribution goes to fund Medicare. The employer and employee both contribute. Currently, the Medicare contribution is 1.45 percent of all wages and salaries, including overtime.

State unemployment tax .... __________

Add this only if the employer contributes.

State disability insurance .... __________

Add this only if the employer contributes.

Worker's compensation insurance .... __________

Determine the amount charged to the employer for Worker's Compensation.

Benefits .... $__________

This is the total amount for all benefits below.

Health insurance .... __________

Justification: Detailed explanation of amount on line

Determine the premium that the employer pays for health insurance. Subtract any employee contribution from the premium. Be sure to include premiums for the entire year.

Dental insurance .... __________

Justification: Detailed explanation of amount on line

Determine the premium that the employer pays for dental insurance. Subtract any employee contribution from the premium. Be sure to include premiums for the entire year.

Life insurance .... __________

Justification: Detailed explanation of amount on line

Determine the premium that the employer pays for life insurance. Subtract any employee contribution from the premium. Be sure to include premiums for the entire year.

Retirement/pension .... __________

Justification: Detailed explanation of amount on line

Determine the premium that the employer pays toward retirement or a pension. This may be based on a percent of wages and salaries. Subtract any employee contribution from the premium. Be sure to include premiums for the entire year.

Office Expenses .... $__________

This is the sum of all of the components below, including rent, utilities, postage, and supplies. Note that office equipment does not include medical training equipment, which is a separate category.

Rent .... $__________

Justification: Detailed explanation of amount on line

This is the annual rent, if any, that is the responsibility of the training section. Rent may be prorated based on space used. For example, if the office rent for the entire agency is $10,000 per month and the office space used by training is 10 percent, then rent for training is $1,000 per month, or $12,000 per year. Find out the total rent for the building and determine the percentage of office spaced used. Your agency may not want any conribution for rent. If so, then enter $0.00 for rent.

Utilities .... $__________

Telephone—Local service .... __________

Include annual local telephone service unless the employer opts to include this service in the agency's monthly telephone bill.

Telephone—Long distance .... __________

Estimate annual long distance telephone calls unless the employer opts to include this service in the agency's monthly telephone bill.

Telephone—Cell phone .... __________

Include service fees for any cellular telephones. Some agencies pay for minute charges while others opt to pay for a monthly plan. There may be a maximum amount the agency is willing to pay for cell phone service. Be sure to calculate costs on an annual basis.

Electric .... __________

Estimate annual electric service unless the employer opts to include this service in the agency's monthly energy bill. Costs can be prorated on a percentage of space used. If the annual electric bill is $10,000 and the training section used 10 percent of the office space, a prorated bill would be $1,000 per year.

Water/sewer .... __________

Estimate annual water and sewer service unless the employer opts to include this service in the agency's monthly bill. Costs can be prorated on a percentage of space used.

Postage .... $__________

Estimate the amount of postage and shipping for the year. If you will be hosting training programs that will be offered to EMTs and paramedics outside the agency, include costs of mailing brochures.

Stationery and supplies .... $__________

State the anticipated costs for office supplies, including pens, paper, notepads, paper clips, tape, etc.

Printing/duplicating .... $__________

Justification: Detailed explanation of amount on line

State the expected costs for printing. Consider any handouts or program materials that will require internal or external copying. Also consider the costs of printing any advertising materials if offering programs to EMS crews not employed by the agency.

Janitorial services .... $__________

Determine who is responsible for cleaning the office and indicate the costs for janitorial services. This may be included at no cost by the agency. If so, state $0.00

Office equipment .... $__________

Justification: Detailed explanation of amount on line

Include any major office equipment such as desks, chairs, computers, printers, copiers, etc. that will be purchased. It might be helpful to capitalize the purchase over a period of time. For example, capitalizing a $3,000 computer over five years means that each year the budget will include $600 for the computer. The equipment budget looks smaller because the cost is spread over time.

Office equipment repair .... $__________

Justification: Detailed explanation of amount on line

Consider expenses if major office equipment needs repair. Service contracts are the least expensive; however, not all items can be covered under a service contract. If a computer malfunctions and needs repair, that cost needs to be budgeted. As with capital office expenditures, major repairs can be budgeted over time, reducing the initial expense.

Travel and Entertainment .... $________

This line represents the total of all travel and entertainment-related expenses. Travel and entertainment includes business travel for staff and any guest speakers. It does not include educational expenses such as travel, lodging, meals, and course fees incurred at local, regional, or national conferences.

Business travel .... $________

Justification: Detailed explanation of amount on line

Plan for local and regional business meetings. Mileage allowances for business travel should be included here. Use the current IRS allowance for business mileage. Airfare is also included in this section. Further, this also includes transportation costs (mileage or airfare) for guest speakers that may be invited to speak at a sponsored training program.

Business lodging and entertainment .... $________

Justification: Detailed explanation of amount on line

Traveling a substantial distance away from home allows for the inclusion of lodging. If there are trips out of the area, include anticipated expenses for all business-related trips. This also pertains to travel costs incurred by guest speakers if staying out-of-town while speaking at a sponsored training session.

Meals/food .... $________

Justification: Detailed explanation of amount on line

Consider any meals or snacks that will be provided at training programs. Coffee, tea, cookies, doughnuts, etc. need to be included in this section. In addition, any meals incurred by guest speakers need to be included in this category as well.

Dues and Subscriptions .... $________

This line represents the total of any association dues, subscription fees, and textbook costs. Subscriptions and textbooks can be used to enhance the training library and benefit the whole organization.

Dues .... $________

Justification: Detailed explanation of amount on line

Dues are any membership fees for professional organizations. Include all organizations, such as the National Association of Emergency Medical Technicians (NAEMT), the National Association of Emergency Medical Services and Educators (NAEMSE), and their respective annual dues.

Periodicals .... $________

Justification: Detailed explanation of amount on line

List all subscriptions to trade journals, such as *EMS Magazine, JEMS* (*Journal of Emergency Medical Services*), etc. Multiple subscriptions, that is, a copy of a magazine for each station, also need to be included.

Textbooks and training aids .... $________

Justification: Detailed explanation of amount on line

If planning to buy any textbooks (including updated editions) or training slide programs, list all textbooks or programs and their costs. Be sure to include a reasonable fee for shipping, handling, and sales tax.

Education and Training .... $________

Travel costs that are incurred for training, such as expenses for attending conferences, are included on this line.

Travel .... $__________

Justification: Detailed explanation of amount on line

Plan to attend local, regional, and national training seminars. Mileage allowances for travel to these conferences should be included here. Use the current IRS allowance for business mileage. Airfare to attend these seminars is also included in this section. This section does not include costs for guest speakers at sponsored programs.

Lodging .... $__________

Justification: Detailed explanation of amount on line

Traveling to attend a conference over several days usually includes the costs of overnight lodging. If there are trips out of the area, include anticipated expenses for all business-related trips. This also pertains to travel costs incurred by staff only to attend educational conferences and seminars.

Meals away from home .... $__________

Justification: Detailed explanation of amount on line

Meals are included for overnight conferences or those that are a considerable distance away from home. Meals include breakfast, lunch, and dinner. Most agencies have a spending limit for each meal, such as $5 for breakfast, $10 for lunch, and $20 for dinner. All anticipated meals need to be included.

Course fees .... $__________

Justification: Detailed explanation of amount on line

Include any registration fees for training conferences. You may want to list each conference separately with its respective fee, then total the amount for the line.

Equipment .... $__________

Equipment expenses include purchases of major training aids such as mannikins, slides, projectors, other training aids, and vehicles. As with capital expenditures for office equipment, major purchases can be capitalized over a period of time.

Training equipment .... $__________

- Mannikins .... __________
- Projectors .... __________
- Soft goods for training (disposable) .... __________
- Repairs and maintenance .... __________

Vehicle equipment .... $__________

- Purchased .... __________
- Leased .... __________
- Gas, tires, oil .... __________
- Insurance .... __________
- Repairs and maintenance .... __________

Once all of the costs have been identified for each major category, add all of the costs to determine a training section budget. If the budget seems excessive, carefully look at each category and identify those areas that can be reduced. A strong hint is in order: Do not present the leanest budget at the first meeting. If the initial budget is too tight, cutting it might result in a budget that is not workable. Allow for some flexibility in your budget.

EXAMPLE OF A COMPLETED WORKSHEET

Following is the same form, less the explanations, that has been completed for a sample budget. It is not reflective of all training programs in every EMS agency, but it serves as an illustration of the figures that need to be included.

Personnel Expenses **$136,916**

Wages and salaries $100,000

Justification: 2 FTO @ $40,000 each and 1 administrative assistant @ $20,000

Overtime $2,000

Justification: FTO on salary—10% of base for administrative assistant

COLA $2,000

Justification: COLA @ 2%—$100,000 × 0.02

Payroll taxes $20,676

FICA (6.2% × $104,000) 6,448

Medicare (1.45% × $104,000) 1,508

State unemployment tax (1.5% × $104,000) 1,560

State disability insurance (1.5% × $104,000) 1,560

Worker's compensation insurance ($800/mo × 12) 9,600

Benefits $12,240

Health insurance 9,540

Justification: $265/mo × 3 employees × 12 mo

Dental insurance 540

Justification: $15/mo × 3 employees × 12 mo

Life insurance $360

Justification: $10/mo × 3 employees × 12 mo

Retirement/pension $1,800

Justification: $50/mo × 3 employees × 12 mo

Office Expenses **$22,711**

Rent $12,000

Justification: $10,000/mo × 10% × 12 mo

Utilities $936

Telephone—local service .... included in rent

Telephone—long distance .... included in rent

Telephone—cell phone, $39/mo × 2 × 12 mo $936

Electricity .... included in rent

Water/sewer .... included in rent

Postage $150

Stationery and supplies $500

Printing/duplicating $1,500

Justification: Program handouts for 12 monthly sessions

Janitorial services (included in rent) $0

Office equipment $6,245

Justification: Laptop computer and software $3,500
Desks (2) @ $350 each (1 FTO in field)
Chairs (2) @ $200 each
File cabinets (1) @ $150 each
Copier @ $1,495 each

Office equipment repair $1,200

Justification: Estimated @ $100/mo

Travel and Entertainment **$1,048.40**

Business travel $413.40

Justification: Travel to state EMS council, 190 mi × $0.36/mi
Travel for guest speaker at seminar—airline, $345

Business lodging and entertainment $100

Justification: Lodging for guest speaker @ $100/night × 1 night

Meals/Food $535

Justification: Meals for guest speaker @ $35 per diem, coffee and tea for breaks at seminar @ $5/person × 100 participants

Dues and Subscriptions **$903.92**

Dues $105

Justification: NAEMSE dues ($65), NAEMT dues ($40)

Periodicals $48.92

Justification: EMS Magazine ($19.95), JEMS ($28.97)

Textbooks and training aids $750

Justification: AAOS ($75), MedEMT ($85), Paramedic Care ($190), Geriatric Prehospital Care ($28), Anatomy & Physiology for Emergency Care ($50), Medical Terminology with Human Anatomy ($50), Stedman's Medical Dictionary ($50), others—to be determined

Education and Training **$975.80**

Travel $245.80

Justification: Travel to Las Vegas ($195), parking @ $10/day × 4 days, mileage to airport @ 30 miles × 0.36/mile

Lodging $330

Justification: Lodging @ EMS Expo @ $110/night × 3 nights

Meals away from home $105

Justification: Meals @ $35 per diem × 3 days

Course fees $295

Justification: EMS Expo ($295)

Equipment **$15,510**

Training equipment $5,860

Mannikins $3,065

Justification: Adult CPR @ $495 × 2, Child CPR @ $575 × 2, Infant CPR @ $425 × 1

CPR mannikin supplies including lungs, wipes, and faces @ $500

Projectors—1 multimedia projector @ $2,195 each $2,195

Soft goods for training (disposable) $500

Repairs and maintenance (estimated) $100

Vehicle equipment $9,650

Purchased $0

Leased @ $300/mo × 12 mo $3,600

Gas, tires, oil @ $0.20/mi × 15,000 miles $3,000

Insurance $650/year $650

Repairs and maintenance @ $0.16/mi × 15,000 miles $2,400

Total Budget **$178,065.12**

SUMMARY

Budget development can be lengthy and tedious. Figures must be checked and verified. Once submitted, the budget is subject to revision, especially reduction. However, developing a budget will give a true illustration of the costs involved with training.

In Closing

Looking at the Role of the Field Training Officer

By now, you are probably amazed at what your role will be as a field training officer (and, maybe, you are wondering if you still want to be an FTO!). As an FTO, you will wear many "hats." Some will include:

* Teacher
* Evaluator
* Counselor
* Advisor
* Mentor
* Coach
* Performance consultant

While wearing these hats, you will provide assistance to new employees as they become familiar with the policies, procedures, and operations of your employer. Your functions will include:

* Instructing
* Critiquing
* Refreshing
* Reinforcing

You will be an integral part of the orientation and training process for new employees. In addition, you might also be called upon to assist other employees. Finally, you will also be called upon to assist in training all company employees. But there is still something else to consider . . .

SUMMARY

This section, "On Being a Teacher," has given you some insight into teaching, including the methods involved in sharing the knowledge and skills you have acquired over the years in emergency medical services. Some of the basic principles of teaching have been addressed, including the differences between teaching children (pedagogy) and teaching adults (andragogy).

You have also been given some information regarding the tools of the trade, such as objectives and lesson plans. One important tool the field training officer will use is the written evaluation. Performance evaluation review forms as well as skills performance sheets have been included in the Appendix for your review or use.

Being a field training officer is a unique opportunity for you. It takes dedication and hard work, but the rewards are tremendous.

Welcome to Training!

APPENDIX A

Sample Lesson Plans

Sample of Outline Format

INTRODUCTION

Goal and Objectives for Introduction

Goal
At the end of the Introduction, the student will understand the nature, scope, and time frame of the field training officer program.

Objectives
At the end of the Introduction, the student will be able to:

1. State one reason why the field training officer program is being offered.
2. List four sections of the program.
3. State the days and times the class will meet.
4. State who authored the paragraph called "The Skillful Teacher."
5. State what Confucius means by leading, strengthening, and opening the way.

I. INTRODUCTION

A. Welcome

B. Purpose of the Course
   1. What
   2. How
   3. Why

C. Course Topics and Schedule
   1. Section I—The Art of Being Human
      a. Tuesday evening
      b. Understanding human behavior
         (1) Personality quizzes
         (2) Understanding yourself
         (3) Understanding others
      c. Help in teaching
      d. Help in communicating
      e. Help in motivating
   2. Section II—Communications
      a. Thursday evening
      b. Various aspects of interpersonal communications
         (1) Help in understanding others
         (2) Help in others understanding you
         (3) Help in teaching and motivating
   3. Section III—Management
      a. Sunday morning
      b. Various aspects of managing others
         (1) FTO is part of field
         (2) FTO is part of management
      c. Help for motivating others
      d. Hints for effective supervision
   4. Section IV—On Being a Teacher
      a. Sunday morning and afternoon
      b. Principles of education
         (1) How people learn
         (2) Adult education
         (3) Motivating the adult learner
         (4) Hints for evaluating others
      c. The PER
         (1) Discuss
         (2) Revise
         (3) Finalize
      d. Skills evaluations

D. "The Skillful Teacher," by Confucius

When a superior man knows the causes which make instruction successful, and those which make it of no effect, he can become a teacher of others. Thus, in his teaching, he leads and does not drag; he strengthens and does not discourage; he opens the way but does not conduct to the end without the learner's own efforts. Leading, and not dragging, produces harmony. Strengthening and not discouraging makes attainment easy. Opening the way and not conducting to the end makes the learner thoughtful. He who produces such harmony, easy attainment, and thoughtfulness may be pronounced a skillful teacher.

Field Training Officer Sample Leader's Guide

PURPOSE OF THE LEADER'S GUIDE

The purpose of this Leader's Guide is to assist the facilitator in preparing and delivering a training session for the field training officer. The guide consists of a preparatory section to aid in getting ready for the training session and a delivery section that facilitates presentation of the material.

TRAINING SESSION PREPARATION

In preparing for the presentation, the instructor will need to ensure adequate training facilities, equipment, and handout materials.

Facilities Needed

The training session can be conducted in a formal classroom or conference room that has adequate seating for all participants. Minimal requirements for the facility include:

- Tables and chairs
- Instructor table for multimedia or overhead projector
- Projection screen or blank, white wall to show slides or overheads

Prerequisites for Participants

Company employee for a minimum of one year, certification as EMT or greater.

Equipment Needed

The following equipment will be needed:

- Multimedia or overhead projector
- Pad and easel
- Marking pens
- Masking tape to attach charts to wall

Materials Needed

Materials to be used in the training session include:

- Leader's Guide
- Participant Handout for reference
    - Copies of slides
    - Copy of Transitional Care form
    - Copy of precertification list
- Overheads

TRAINING SESSION DELIVERY

The training session delivery will consist of two sections, "Opening," and "Delivery." (Only the first section is included in the sample here.)

Opening

Welcome participants to the field training officer training program.

Introduce self and coinstructors, if any.
Have participants introduce selves especially if they are from diverse areas of the region or from multiple regions.

Share the goal of the session. It is to become familiar with the role and functions of the field training officer. Specifically, this section, "Introduction," is geared to the nature, scope, and time frame of the program.

Ask what the benefits that can be gained from knowing about education and the roles of the FTO are.

Review program objectives using overheads.

Explain that upon completion of the program, the participant will be able to:

- State one reason why the program is being offered.
- List four sections of the program.
- State the length of the class. If longer than one day, state the days and times the class will meet.
- State the author of the paragraph called "The Skillful Teacher."
- Understand what is meant by the phrase in the statement, "leading, strengthening, and opening the way."

APPENDIX B

Sample Skills Checklists

Diagnostic Signs

Performance Objective

To be able to successfully take and record a patient's blood pressure, pulse, and respiratory rate

Name: ______________________ Date: __________ P F

Scorer: ______________________ Date: __________ P F

Passing criteria: All steps with © are critical and must be passed. No more than 4 points missed overall (80%).

	Score	
1. Palpated Blood Pressure		
A. Apply blood pressure cuff 1 inch above antecubital fossa	©	©
1. Snug fit		
2. Center bladder over artery		
B. Palpate radial or brachial pulse	©	©
C. Inflate cuff to 10 mm Hg above point where pulse ceases	1	1
D. Deflate cuff and determine palpable blood pressure (+/− 4 mm Hg)	©	©
2. Auscultated Blood Pressure		
A. Apply blood pressure cuff as above	©	©
B. Palpate brachial artery	2	2
C. Inflate cuff	1	1
D. Place diaphragm of stethoscope over brachial artery (May be done before inflating cuff)	1	1
E. Deflate cuff and determine auscultated blood pressure (+/− 4 mm Hg)	©	©
3. Radial/Brachial Pulse		
A. Do not use thumb to palpate pulse	3	3
B. Take pulse for 15 seconds and multiply by 4	2	2
C. Determine pulse rate (+/− 4 beats/minute)		

(continued)

4. Respiration		
A. Watch rise and fall of chest/abdomen for 30 seconds and multiply by 2	2	2
B. Determine respiratory rate (+/− 2/minutes)	©	©
5. Skin Signs		
A. Observe skin color for cyanosis, jaundice, pallor, or flushing	©	©
B. Observe skin condition	©	©
1. Touch patient with back of hand		
2. Note temperature (warm, cool, hot)		
3. Note moisture (dry, damp, diaphoretic)		
6. Level of Consciousness		
A. Evaluate patient's response	©	©
1. Alert		
2. Responds to verbal stimuli		
3. Responds to physical stimuli		
4. No response		
7. Neurological Examination		
A. Observe eye opening	©	©
1. Open spontaneously		
2. To verbal command		
3. To physical stimuli		
4. No response		
B. Determine best verbal response	©	©
1. If able to communicate, ask:		
a. What is your name?	2	2
b. Where are you?	2	2
c. What time of day is it?	2	2
2. Response	©	©
a. Alert and oriented—converses		
b. Disoriented and converses		
c. Inappropriate words		
d. Incomprehensible sounds		
e. No response		
C. Determine best motor response	©	©
1. To verbal: obeys		
2. To physical stimulus:		
a. Localizes		
b. Withdraws		
c. Flexion response		
d. Extension response		
e. No response		
D. Determine pupil size and reaction	©	©
1. Look at both eyes for equality and pupil size		
2. Check for reaction to light		
a. Shine light in each eye, approaching from periphery		
b. In daylight, cover eye with hand, removing to let light in		
3. Student states size and reaction of pupils	©	©

Comments: ____

____

____

Patient Evaluation

Performance Objective

To be able to successfully perform a thorough patient evaluation

Name: ______________________ Date: ____________ P F

Scorer: ______________________ Date: ____________ P F

Passing criteria: All steps with © are critical and must be passed.
No more than 8 points missed overall (80%).

	Score	
1. Primary Survey		
A. Global survey (student states presence or absence of the following):	©	©
1. Environmental dangers		
2. Number of victims		
3. Need for additional resources		
4. Mechanism of injury		
5. Need for extrication		
B. Assess victim's airway and breathing (identify self to conscious patient and ask permission to treat):	©	©
1. Check for noisy, gurgling, or snoring respiration		
2. If unconscious, shake and shout		
3. Correct any airway deficits	©	©
a. Open airway by appropriate method. Use C-spine precautions if necessary		
4. Check for spontaneous respiration	©	©
a. State whether normal, shallow, deep, or labored		
b. If unconscious, look, listen, and feel		
5. Correct any severe breathing difficulties	©	©
a. Treat potential life-threatening problems		
(1) Sucking chest wound—apply occlusive dressing		
(2) Flailing chest—stabilize		
b. Ventilate if needed	©	©
(1) Supplemental oxygen		
(2) Oro- or nasopharyngeal airway		
C. Assess circulation:	©	©
1. Palpate pulse: carotid pulse if unconscious		
2. Note skin signs		
3. Assess for life-threatening bleeding	©	©
4. Correct any circulation problems	©	©
a. Initiate CPR if needed	©	©
b. If life threatening, control external bleeding	©	©
D. Evaluate level of consciousness.	©	©
E. Determine if immediate transport is needed:	©	©
1. State "If victim has evidence of a life-threatening emergency, then transport immediately with further assessment and treatment en route."		
2. Secondary Survey		
A. Obtain chief complaint:	©	©
1. Why was help requested? What hurts the most?		
2. What caused it? (P)		
3. How would you describe the problem or pain? (Q)		
4. In what region is the pain—any radiation? (R)		
5. What is its severity? (Use 1–10 scale) (S)		
6. How long has pain/problem persisted? (T)		
B. If trauma, determine mechanism of injury.	©	©
C. Determine if the patient lost consciousness.	©	©
D. Obtain history:	©	©
1. Are you under doctor's care?		

(*continued*)

2. Do you have any medical problems?		
3. Do you take medications?		
4. Are you allergic to anything?		
5. How old are you?		
E. Obtain vital signs (may be done after head-to-toe survey):	©	©
1. Blood pressure	©	©
2. Pulse rate and quality	©	©
3. Respiratory rate and quality	©	©
F. Head-to-toe survey (maintain spinal precautions if necessary):		
1. Head		
a. Scalp: palpate with both hands, looking for hematomas, depressions, active bleeding	2	2
b. Nose and ears: palpate for deformity, check for blood fluid or drainage	3	3
c. Facial bones and mouth: palpate for pain, deformity; inspect for loose teeth, blood, secretions, obstructions, dentures, hydration, and tongue lacerations	3	3
d. Check pupils for size and reaction	3	3
2. C-spine: palpate for pain, deformity, must not move head	©	©
3. Neck: observe for tracheal deviation, Medic-Alert, JVD	2	2
4. Chest		
a. Inspect for bilateral chest rise, bruises, scars, penetrations, paradoxical movement, barrel chest	2	2
b. Palpate lateral chest walls with deep inspiration for pain or deformity; sternum with side of hand	2	2
c. Auscultate for bilateral breath sounds anterior at midclavicular line at level of midsternum; posterior at axillary line for lung bases; state findings	2	2
5. Abdomen		
a. Inspect for bruising, scars, penetrations, eviscerations, or distention	2	2
b. Palpate gently over all four quadrants, one at a time, for pain, guarding, rigidity, or rebound tenderness	2	2
6. Thoraco-lumbar spine		
a. Without lifting or moving the patient, palpate as much of the thoraco-lumbar spine as possible, checking for pain, deformity, or bleeding	2	2
7. Pelvis		
a. Gently compress the pelvis posteriorally and medially to check for pain or crepitus; check for incontinence	2	2
8. Lower extremities (one at a time)		
a. Palpate thigh, knee, and calf for pain or deformity; observe for bruises, lacerations, open fractures	2	2
b. Inspect and palpate for pedal edema, trauma	2	2
c. Inspect and palpate feet for CMSTP	3	3
9. Upper extremities (check one at a time)		
a. Clavicle, scapula, and shoulder girdle: palpate for pain and deformity	2	2
b. Arms: palpate for pain and deformity, observe for needle marks or bruises	2	2
c. Wrists: palpate for trauma and pulses, check for equality of pulses	2	2
d. Hands: check CMSTP	3	3
10. Back		
a. Logroll patient and observe for bruises, scars, entrance/exit wounds; palpate entire thoracic and lumbar spine for pain and deformity	©	©

Comments: ____

____

____

Airway Management

Performance Objective

To demonstrate the proper airway control using oro- and nasopharyngeal airways, the bag–valve-mask device, demand valve device, and proper oro- and nasopharyngeal suctioning techniques

Name: ______________________ Date: __________ P F

Scorer: ______________________ Date: __________ P F

Passing criteria: All steps are critical and must be passed.

	Score	
1. Oropharyngeal Airway		
A. Determine unconsciousness: attempt to verbally or physically stimulate the patient.	©	©
B. Determine appropriate-sized airway: measure to airway from corner of mouth to bottom of ear.	©	©
C. Insert airway: insert with tip toward roof of mouth until it passes top of tongue, then rotate 180 degrees and seat into position.	©	©
D. Check for responsiveness: remove airway if patient shows signs of gagging, retching, or awakening.	©	©
E. Reassess ventilation: look, listen, and feel for adequate air exchange; ventilate as needed.	©	©
2. Nasopharyngeal Airway		
A. Determine appropriate-sized airway: measure from tip of nose to bottom of ear; use airway that is slightly smaller in diameter than the patient's nostrils.	©	©
B. Insert airway: lubricate airway with water-soluble lubricant; insert at slight angle upward toward patient's forehead; guide gently until flange is resting on nostril.	©	©
C. Reassess ventilation: look, listen, and feel for adequate air exchange; ventilate as needed.	©	©
3. Suctioning (Rigid or Flexible Suction Catheter)		
A. Prepare equipment: connect catheter and extension tubing to suction unit. Activate and test unit for suction power.	©	©
B. Determine depth to insert catheter: measure from corner of mouth to bottom of ear (oropharyngeal suctioning) or tip of nose to bottom of ear (nasopharyngeal suction).	©	©
C. Proceed with suctioning: insert catheter to appropriate depth; occlude vent to start suction; withdraw catheter while twisting. **Suction no longer than 5 seconds.** If patient vomits, put in left lateral position and finger sweep.	©	©
4. Basic Oxygen Delivery		
A. Attach regulator: connect regulator to oxygen tank.	©	©
B. Assure oxygen supply: open tank; check gauge for adequate pressure and absence of leaks.	©	©
C. Apply nasal cannula: attach end of tubing to regulator and adjust flow to 2–6 liters per minute; place prongs in nostrils, secure tubing over ears, and tighten under chin.	©	©
D. Apply simple face mask: attach end of tubing to regulator and adjust flow to 6–10 liters per minute. Place mask over mouth and nose and adjust strap to ensure snug fit.	©	©
E. Apply nonrebreather mask: attach end of tubing to regulator and adjust flow to 10–15 liters per minute. Fill reservoir bag	©	©

(*continued*)

by occluding diaphragm. Place mask over mouth and nose and ensure a snug fit.

5. Bag–Valve–Mask Operation
   A. Open oxygen regulator and ensure adequate pressure. © ©
   B. Connect supplemental oxygen tubing to regulator and device. © ©
   C. Turn on regulator and adjust flow rate to 15 liters per minute. © ©
   D. Apply mask: with one hand, obtain tight seal while maintaining proper head/jaw position. © ©
   E. Ventilate at a rate of at least 12 times per minute. © ©
   F. Assess effectiveness by watching rise and fall of chest. © ©
6. Demand valve/Positive Pressure Resuscitator
   A. Open oxygen regulator and ensure adequate pressure. Close liter flow control. © ©
   B. Secure mask to face and ensure tight seal using both hands while maintaining proper airway control. © ©
   C. Ventilate at a rate of 12 times per minute by using thumb to trigger oxygen delivery. Avoid overinflation. © ©
   D. Assess effectiveness by watching rise and fall of chest. © ©

Comments: ____

____

____

____

Spinal Immobilization: Long Board

Performance Objective
To properly immobilize a patient onto a long spine board

Name: ____________________ Date: __________ P F

Scorer: ____________________ Date: __________ P F

Passing criteria: All steps with © are critical and must be passed.
No more than 1 point missed overall (80%).

	Score	
1. Explain procedure to patient.	1	1
2. Explain procedure to assistant.	2	2
3. Direct assistant to apply and maintain immobilization to head.	©	©
4. Conduct CMSTP of arms and legs.	3	3
5. Size and apply rigid cervical collar without moving head.	©	©
6. Direct assistant to position long spine board and properly position assistants to logroll patient as a unit, maintaining alignment at all times.	©	©
7. Center patient on long spine board and secure patient with straps across torso, hips, and legs so that patient will not move if placed on left side.	©	©
8. Secure head to board using tape and towels or Head Bed device.	©	©
9. Direct assistant to release manual C-spine immobilization.	1	1
10. Conduct CMSTP of arms and legs.	©	©
11. Immobilization will not vary more than 10 degrees when patient is placed in left lateral position.	©	©

Comments: ____

Application of Kendrick Extrication Device (K.E.D.)

Performance Objective

To properly immobilize a patient using a short spine board or K.E.D.

Name: ____________________ Date: __________ P F

Scorer: ____________________ Date: __________ P F

Passing criteria: All steps with © are critical and must be passed.
No more than 3 points missed overall (80%).

	Score	
1. Explain procedure to patient.	1	1
2. Immobilize and support head.	©	©
3. Ask for assistance, explain procedures, and direct assistant to maintain manual immobilization.	1	1
4. Check arms and legs for CMSTP.	©	©
5. Size and apply cervical collar.	©	©
6. Ease K.E.D. behind patient, ensure snug fit under axillary region.	©	©
7. Secure torso straps.	3	3
8. Secure leg straps.	3	3
9. Apply padding behind neck if needed.	2	2
10. Secure patient's head, forehead first, to K.E.D. using straps or tape.	©	©
11. Do not flex or extend head more than 10 degrees.	©	©
12. State or demonstrate that patient's hands will be tied to restrict movement.	1	1
13. Instruct assistant to place long board in position.	2	2
14. Control patient while turning.	©	©
15. Lay patient on long board with legs flexed.	2	2
16. Loosen but do not release leg straps.	3	3
17. Extend legs for comfort.	1	1
18. Secure patient to long board using straps.	©	©
19. Secure patient's head to long board using towel rolls and tape or Head Bed.	©	©
20. Reassess CMSTP in all extremities.	©	©
21. Immobilization should prevent flexion/extension by more than 10 degrees and lateral movement of the head by one-half inch.	©	©
22. If patient vomits, turn patient onto left side to clear and protect airway.	©	©

Comments: ____

Bandaging and Splinting of an Open Fracture of the Tibia/Radius

Performance Objective

To properly immobilize an open fracture of the tibia and/or radius

Name: ____________________ Date: __________ P F

Scorer: ____________________ Date: __________ P F

Passing criteria: All steps with © are critical and must be passed.
No more than 4 points missed overall (80%).

	Score	
1. Explain procedure to patient.	1	1
2. Expose extremity.	2	2
3. Instruct assistant to stabilize extremity without applying traction and provide support under the fracture site.	©	©
4. Remove shoe and sock from injured leg (if leg fracture).	3	3
5. Check CMSTP of the extremity.	©	©
6. Apply sterile dressing to wound and secure without applying pressure over the exposed bone.	©	©
7. Select appropriate-sized rigid splint by measuring beside extremity; must be long enough to immobilize joint above and below injury.	©	©
8. Pad splint as needed before application.	2	2
9. Slide splint under extremity.	2	2
10. Secure splint to extremity using cravats being sure not to cover fracture site but to immobilize joint above and below injury.	©	©
11. If arm fracture, apply sling for support.	3	3
12. Recheck CMSTP.	©	©
13. Splint should be applied so as to prevent movement at fracture site and at proximal and distal joints by no more than half inch.	©	©

Comments: ____

Traction Splint: Hare

Performance Objective

To properly immobilize a closed fracture of the femur using a Hare traction splint

Name: ______________________ Date: __________ P F

Scorer: ______________________ Date: __________ P F

Passing criteria: *All steps with © are critical and must be passed.*
No more than 4 points missed overall (80%).

	Score	
1. Explain procedure to patient.	1	1
2. State, "I will expose leg and visualize fracture site."	2	2
3. Remove patient's shoe and sock.	3	3
4. Check CMSTP of injured leg.	©	©
5. Measure splint for proper length using uninjured leg.	3	3
5. Apply ankle hitch and have assistant initiate manual traction by grasping straps on ankle hitch (not D-rings).	©	©
6. Place splint under fractured leg, pushing top under ischium.	©	©
7. Secure groin strap.	3	3
8. Attach ankle hitch to splint and apply mechanical traction, then raise foot stand.	©	©
9. Instruct assistant to release manual traction.	3	3
10. Secure Velcro supports (two above and two below the knee).	3	3
11. Recheck CMSTP of injured leg.	©	©
12. Upon completion, leg must be immobilized to prevent movement.	©	©

Comments: ____

Traction Splint: Sager

Performance Objective

To properly immobilize a closed fracture of the femur using a Sager traction splint

Name: ______________________ Date: ____________ P F

Scorer: ______________________ Date: ____________ P F

Passing criteria: All steps with © are critical and must be passed.
No more than 3 points missed overall (80%).

	Score	
1. Explain procedure to patient.	1	1
2. State, "I will expose leg and visualize the fracture site."	2	2
3. Remove the patient's shoe and sock.	3	3
4. Check CMSTP of injured leg.	©	©
5. Measure Sager splint for proper length using uninjured leg and measuring from groin to just below heel.	©	©
6. Instruct assistant to apply and maintain manual traction.	©	©
7. Place uninjured leg in a position that will not interfere with splint.	1	1
8. Place padded upper portion of splint against groin area.	©	©
9. Secure groin strap.	3	3
10. Measure, adjust, and secure ankle hitch.	©	©
11. Apply traction based on 10 percent of patient's body weight.	©	©
12. Instruct assistant to release manual traction.	2	2
13. Immobilize knee joint by placing straps above and over knee joint.	3	3
14. Prevent lateral rotation by securing injured leg to uninjured leg with strap tied in a figure eight around ankles and feet.	1	1
15. Elevate extremity if possible.	1	1
16. Recheck CMSTP.	©	©
17. Upon completion, limb must be immobilized to prevent movement.	©	©

Comments: ____

Application of a Sling and Swathe

Performance Objective

To properly immobilize a closed fracture of the arm using a sling and swathe

Name: ______________________ Date: __________ P F

Scorer: ______________________ Date: __________ P F

Passing criteria: All steps with © are critical and must be passed.
No more than 4 points missed overall (80%).

	Score	
1. Explain procedure to patient.	1	1
2. Check CMSTP of injured extremity.	©	©
3. Have patient support forearm at waist level (position of comfort).	2	2
4. Place base of sling under wrist with one end over the shoulder.	2	2
5. Place lower end of base over forearm and shoulder.	2	2
6. Tie ends together around neck.	2	2
7. Bring apex around elbow and secure with safety pin.	2	2
8. Place swathe over injured arm, under opposite arm, and wrap around body. Secure so that arm is immobilized against chest wall.	©	©
9. Recheck CMSTP of injured extremity.	©	©
10. On completion, limb should be immobilized to prevent movement.	©	©

Comments: ____

Assisting in Normal/Abnormal Delivery of an Infant

Performance Objective

To demonstrate proper procedures used in the prehospital delivery of a neonate, as well as handle unexpected complications of childbirth and perform an APGAR score of the newborn

Name: ______________________ Date: __________ P F

Scorer: ______________________ Date: __________ P F

Passing criteria: All steps with © are critical and must be passed. No more than 7 points missed overall (80%).

	Score	
1. Introduce self and ask permission to examine and treat.	1	1
2. Determine whether to transport or prepare for delivery by asking:		
A. When is your baby due?	2	2
B. How many babies have you had?	2	2
C. Has your bag of water broken?	2	2
D. When did your contractions start?	2	2
E. How far apart are your contractions?	2	2
F. Do you feel the need to move your bowels or bear down?	2	2
G. Does your doctor expect any complications with this delivery?	2	2
3. Position mother supine with legs apart and bent	2	2
4. Explain need and ask permission to check for crowning or bulging perineum	3	3
5. If delivery imminent, open OB kit.	1	1
6. Put on nonsterile gloves, cleanse perineum from top to bottom, and drape mother.	2	2
7. Remove nonsterile gloves and put on sterile gloves using aseptic technique.	3	3
8. Normal or abnormal delivery (if abnormal conditions, see section below):		
A. Place one hand on baby's head and use other hand to prevent explosive delivery.	©	©
B. After head delivers, clear airway by suctioning mouth and nose with bulb syringe (squeeze air out of syringe before inserting).	©	©
C. Apply gentle downward pressure to deliver upper shoulder.	2	2
D. Apply gentle upward pressure to deliver lower shoulder.	2	2
E. After delivery, resuction mouth and nose as in Step B above.	©	©
F. If baby is not breathing, rub back briskly and flick soles of feet to stimulate breathing.	©	©
G. Wrap baby in warm blanket to maintain warmth, ensuring baby's head is covered.	©	©
H. After cord stops pulsating, clamp cord at least six to eight inches from baby and again four inches from first clamp while keeping baby below level of mother's heart.	©	©
I. Place baby on mother's abdomen or breast.	1	1
J. Deliver and examine placenta, then place in plastic bag and put on baby to maintain warmth.	3	3
K. Massage fundus of uterus and place sanitary napkin over vaginal opening.	©	©
9. Perform APGAR score on baby at 1 and 5 minutes after birth.	©	©

(*continued*)

10. Abnormal delivery options: evaluator may substitute one of the following abnormal conditions:		
A. Cord wrapped loosely around infant's neck		
1. Attempt to slip cord over infant's head or manually loosen.	©	©
B. Cord wrapped tightly around infant's neck		
1. Clamp and cut cord after attempting to manually loosen.	©	©
C. Breech delivery		
1. Insert gloved hand (two fingers at bottom of vaginal opening) to provide airway for baby.	©	©
2. Indicate this is a Code 3 transport.	©	©
D. Failure of amniotic sac to rupture		
1. Tear the sac and remove from infant's airway.	©	©
E. Prolapsed cord		
1. Insert gloved hand to relieve pressure on cord.	©	©
2. Properly position mother.	©	©
3. Indicate this is a Code 3 transport.	©	©

Comments: ____

____

____

____

Administration of Oral Glucose

Performance Objective

To demonstrate the administration of oral glucose to a hypoglycemic patient

Name: ______________________ Date: __________ P F

Scorer: ______________________ Date: __________ P F

Passing criteria: All steps are critical and must be passed.

	Score	
1. Explain procedure to patient.	1	1
2. Check medication for accuracy and expiration date.	©	©
3. Using tongue depressor, place glucose paste between cheek and gum or under tongue.	©	©
4. Place patient in left lateral position to prevent aspiration and have suction available.	©	©
5. Monitor airway and level of consciousness.	©	©

Comments: ____

____

____

____

Lifting and Moving Patients

Performance Objective

To demonstrate proper lifting and moving techniques using the two-person extremities carry, two-person direct carry, draw-sheet, and scoop stretcher

Name: ____________________ Date: __________ P F

Scorer: ____________________ Date: __________ P F

Passing criteria: All steps with © are critical and must be passed.
No more than 9 points missed overall (80%).

	Score	
1. Two-Person Lift (Extremities Carry or Sit/Pick)		
A. Approach patient, one from behind and one from the feet.	2	2
B. Student at feet grasps patient's hands or shoulders and raises patient to sitting position (done after full examination is completed).	3	3
C. Student in back kneels and grasps patient under both arms and secures patient's hands with his/her hands across patient's chest.	2	2
D. Student at feet, standing to one side, places his/her hands under patient's legs.	2	2
F. Patient is lifted and positioned on gurney.	3	3
2. Two-Person Lift—Bed to Stretcher—Direct Carry		
A. Head end of stretcher is placed at foot end of bed.	2	2
B. Put patient in supine position.	2	2
C. Student at patient's head places arm under patient's neck and other arm under patient's back.	2	2
D. Second student places arm under patient's hips and other arm under patient's calves.	2	2
E. Patient is slid to edge of bed.	2	2
F. Students lift patient and curl patient toward their chests.	3	3
G. Patient is lifted and positioned on gurney.	2	2
3. Draw Sheet Method with Gurney		
A. Loosen bottom sheet under patient.	2	2
B. Position stretcher touching, and at same height as bed.	2	2
C. Reach across stretcher.	2	2
D. Grasp sheet at patient's head, chest, hips, and knees.	2	2
E. Slide patient gently onto stretcher.	3	3
4. Patient Movement—Scoop Stretcher		
A. With patient supine, place scoop alongside patient.	2	2
B. Release bottom pins and extend stretcher to just below soles of patient's feet.	2	2
C. Students position themselves at head and foot ends of scoop and release pins, breaking the stretcher into two halves.	2	2
D. Align both halves on either side of patient without lifting scoop over patient.	2	2
E. Bring both ends of the foot of the stretcher together and lock.	©	©
F. Student at foot end moves to patient's side and gently lifts patient's hips and shoulders, allowing the other student to position the stretcher under patient.	2	2
G. Student at head connects both halves together and locks.	©	©
H. Student at foot end of stretcher repositions him/herself and prepares to lift. Student at head coordinates lift.	2	2
I. Students lift and place patient on gurney.	2	2
J. Students reverse steps to remove patient from scoop stretcher.	2	2

Comments: ____

____

____

____

Treatment of Penetrating Chest Wound: Occlusive Dressing

Performance Objective

To treat the presence of an open chest wound using an occlusive dressing

Name: ______________________	Date: __________	P	F
Scorer: ______________________	Date: __________	P	F

Passing criteria: All steps are critical and must be passed.

	Score	
1. Explain procedure to patient.	©	©
2. Apply petroleum gauze dressing, gauze side down to wound with foil package on top. A. Apply dressing when patient exhales. B. Pad occlusive dressing with several sterile 4 × 4 gauze pads. C. Tape dressing in place on three sides, leaving bottom edge open.	©	©
3. Apply oxygen but do not use positive pressure devices.	©	©
4. Monitor patient for signs of tension pneumothorax.	©	©

Comments: ____

Severe Extremity Bleeding

Performance Objective

To demonstrate proper techniques used in controlling external hemorrhage

Name: ______________________ Date: __________ P F

Scorer: ______________________ Date: __________ P F

Passing criteria: All steps are critical and must be passed.

	Score	
1. Apply direct pressure with pad of 4 × 4 gauze pads or hand.	©	©
2. If dressing becomes saturated, apply more dressings and elevate.	©	©
3. If unable to control, use pressure point to nearest major artery proximal to wound.	©	©
4. If bleeding continues, use BP cuff as tourniquet as last resort.	©	©
A. Apply proximal to wound and not over joint.		
B. Inflate BP cuff to 10 mm Hg above point where bleeding stops.		
5. If BP cuff not available:		
A. Use band at least 3–4 inches wide, placed proximal to wound.	©	©
B. Tie a half knot, center stick, or pen over knot, then tie two knots over stick.	©	©
C. Twist stick to tighten until bleeding stops.	©	©
D. Write TK, time, and place where tourniquet is applied on piece of tape and place tape on patient's forehead.	©	©
6. State, "I would treat the patient for shock, monitor vital signs, and transport Code 3."	©	©

Comments: ____

Stabilizing Impaled Object

Performance Objective
To properly stabilize an impaled object

Name: ______________________ Date: __________ P F

Scorer: ______________________ Date: __________ P F

Passing criteria: All steps are critical and must be passed.

	Score	
1. Explain procedure to patient.	©	©
2. Explain procedure to assistant.	©	©
3. State, "I would expose area around impaled object."	©	©
4. Instruct assistant to grasp object to prevent movement.	©	©
5. Apply gauze pads or bulky dressings around object.	©	©
6. Tape dressings in place to ensure stability.	©	©
7. Impaled object should not move during and after procedure.	©	©

Comments: ____

Measures to Cool Febrile Pediatric Patient

Performance Objective

To demonstrate the ability to use the recommended technique for cooling a child with a high fever

Name: ____________________ Date: __________ P F

Scorer: ____________________ Date: __________ P F

Passing criteria: All steps are critical and must be passed.

	Score	
1. Undress child completely.	©	©
2. Sponge child with tepid water (95–99 degrees—slightly warm to touch) or wrap child in wet sheet.	©	©
3. Begin transport and continue cooling measures.	©	©
4. If child begins shivering, dry child.	©	©

Comments: ______________________________________

Application of Restraints

Performance Objective

Demonstrate the ability to properly apply restraints to a patient involved in a behavioral emergency

Name: ______________________ Date: __________ P F

Scorer: ______________________ Date: __________ P F

Passing criteria: All steps with © must be passed.
No more than 5 points missed overall (70%).

	Score	
1. Select appropriate equipment—complete set of restraints.	3	3
2. Observe and attempt to interact with patient: a. Make effort to gain patient's cooperation. b. Once decision is made to use restraints, move quickly and as a team.	©	©
3. Prepare restraints by opening cuffs and unfastening belts out of sight from patient.	3	3
4. Instruct assistants before approaching. a. Enlist as much manpower as possible. b. Encircle patient. c. One rescuer grasps patient from behind in "bear hug" grip. d. Another rescuer secures patient's head by grasping jaw. e. Another rescuer grasps patient's legs above knees. f. All react in unison.	©	©
5. Instruct assistants by saying, "Now!"	©	©
6. Lower patient to ground.	3	3
7. Secure patient's hands: a. Apply restraints securely. b. Assess circulation distal to restraint.	©	©
8. Secure feet: a. Apply restraints securely. b. Assess circulation distal to restraint.	©	©
9. Place patient onto stretcher and secure restraints to stretcher.	3	3
10. Apply sheet to further secure patient to stretcher.	3	3
11. Assess circulation to hands and feet.	©	©
12. Document procedure: a. Rationale for restraining patient b. Time of application of restraints	3	3

Comments: ____

Airway Management—Pediatrics

Performance Objective

To demonstrate the proper airway control using oropharyngeal airways and the bag–valve–mask device on pediatric patients

Name: ____________________ Date: __________ P F

Scorer: ____________________ Date: __________ P F

Passing criteria: All steps are critical and must be passed.

	Score	
1. Oropharyngeal Airway—Do *not* use on neonates.		
A. Determine unconsciousness: attempt to verbally or physically stimulate the patient.	©	©
B. Determine appropriate-sized airway: measure airway from corner of mouth to bottom of ear.	©	©
C. Insert airway: insert with tip toward roof of mouth until it passes top of tongue, then rotate 180 degrees and seat into position.	©	©
D. Check for responsiveness: remove airway if patient shows signs of gagging, retching, or awakening.	©	©
E. Reassess ventilation: look, listen, and feel for adequate air exchange, ventilate as needed.	©	©
2. Basic Oxygen Delivery		
A. Attach regulator: connect regulator to oxygen tank.	©	©
B. Assure oxygen supply: open tank and check gauge for adequate pressure and absence of leaks.	©	©
C. Apply nasal cannula: attach end of tubing to regulator and adjust flow to 2–6 liters per minute. Place prongs in nostrils, secure tubing over ears, and tighten under chin.	©	©
D. Apply simple face mask: attach end of tubing to regulator and adjust flow to 6–10 liters per minute. Place mask over mouth and nose and adjust strap to ensure snug fit.	©	©
E. Apply nonrebreather mask: attach end of tubing to regulator and adjust flow to 10–15 liters per minute. Fill reservoir bag by occluding diaphragm. Place mask over mouth and nose and ensure a snug fit.	©	©
3. Bag–Valve–Mask Operation		
A. Open oxygen regulator and ensure adequate pressure.	©	©
B. Connect supplemental oxygen tubing to regulator and device.	©	©
C. Turn on regulator and adjust flow rate to 15 liters per minute.	©	©
D. Apply mask: with one hand, obtain tight seal while maintaining proper head/jaw position.	©	©
E. Ventilate at a rate of at least 20 times per minute. Give puffs of air for infants.	©	©
F. Assess effectiveness by watching rise and fall of chest.	©	©

Comments: ____

APPENDIX C

Performance Evaluation Review

The purpose of this employee performance appraisal is to provide an evaluation tool for the newly hired employee to assure his or her progress in learning nonemergency transportation techniques.

This document consists of performance evaluations in the following areas:

- Professional appearance
- Operations procedures and equipment use
- Demonstrated driving ability
- Employee standards
- Patient care
- Documentation

This performance appraisal is an ongoing process and will be reviewed during the initial employment and training period. Additional PERs may be performed at any time.

Performance Evaluation Review

Scoring Guidelines

The criteria below are to be used for scoring the employee or employment candidate during the initial training period or when evaluating the employee's performance annually.

1. **Poor—A score in this range requires written comments**
   Unsatisfactory performance. Could not do skill or does not have knowledge. Will need substantial retraining to master skill or retain knowledge.
2. **Marginal**
   Could perform skill or has basic knowledge. Needed coaching or prompting to complete skill or demonstrate knowledge of written information. Prolonged time required to answer questions or complete skill. In certain categories, new employees may rate a marginal score due to being unfamiliar with policies and procedures of the company.
3. **Average**
   Performed skill with minimal or no coaching but needed to be asked to perform skill. Skill completed within reasonable time. Knowledge base is satisfactory but doesn't understand reasons behind certain policies or procedures.
4. **Commendable**
   Performed skill in minimal amount of time without coaching. Answers questions quickly and without prompting. Above average performance in skills and knowledge.
5. **Superior—A score in this range requires written comments**
   Excellent knowledge and skills base. Performed skills promptly and to the best interest of the patient. Could teach skills to trainee. Knowledge base is sound and understands reasons behind policies and procedures.

N/A **Not Applicable**
The subject or evaluation score does not apply to this employee.

Performance Score Definitions
1 = Poor 2 = Marginal 3 = Average 4 = Commendable 5 = Superior N/A = Not Applicable

Section I Professional Appearance

Employee Name: ______________________ Signature: ____________________

Training Officer: ____________________________ Date: __________________

Performance Criteria	Score (Circle One)					
A. Uniform						
1. Clean, white or pastel shirt	1	2	3	4	5	N/A
2. Clean, dark blue or black pants—no jeans	1	2	3	4	5	N/A
3. Name tag or trainee ID card	1	2	3	4	5	N/A
4. Black boots or shoes, clean/polished	1	2	3	4	5	N/A
5. Dark or white socks	1	2	3	4	5	N/A
6. Solid white T-shirt	1	2	3	4	5	N/A
7. Watch, pen, notepad	1	2	3	4	5	N/A
8. Appropriate earrings (no dangling or hoops)	1	2	3	4	5	N/A
9. Long hair pulled back, out of the way	1	2	3	4	5	N/A
10. Fingernails clean and trimmed	1	2	3	4	5	N/A
B. Personal Hygiene						
1. Well groomed	1	2	3	4	5	N/A
2. Clean and neat overall appearance	1	2	3	4	5	N/A
C. Punctuality						
1. On time and ready to begin shift	1	2	3	4	5	N/A
D. Vehicle						
1. Clean, well-stocked unit at beginning and end of each shift	1	2	3	4	5	N/A
2. Employee demonstrates good time management in cleaning and preparing the unit for service	1	2	3	4	5	N/A

E. Comments:

Performance Score Definitions

1 = Poor 2 = Marginal 3 = Average 4 = Commendable 5 = Superior N/A = Not Applicable

Section II — Operations Procedures
Use of Equipment and Radio

Employee Name: ____________________ Signature: ____________________

Training Officer: ____________________ Date: ____________________

Performance Criteria	Score (Circle One)					
A. Vehicle						
1. Checks vehicle according to driver checklist	1	2	3	4	5	N/A
2. Checks patient area per checklist	1	2	3	4	5	N/A
B. Radio						
1. Understands technical aspects of radio	1	2	3	4	5	N/A
2. Assures radio is in working order	1	2	3	4	5	N/A
3. Understands and uses the 10-code system	1	2	3	4	5	N/A
4. Provides fast, accurate data to dispatch	1	2	3	4	5	N/A
5. Uses calm, clear voice	1	2	3	4	5	N/A
6. Limits traffic to necessary communications	1	2	3	4	5	N/A
C. Lifts						
1. Properly and safely loads patient onto gurney	1	2	3	4	5	N/A
2. Properly and safely loads gurney into ambulance	1	2	3	4	5	N/A
D. Tie-Downs and Straps						
1. Properly secures gurney to ambulance	1	2	3	4	5	N/A
2. Makes sure patient is properly secured	1	2	3	4	5	N/A

E. Comments:

Performance Score Definitions

1 = Poor 2 = Marginal 3 = Average 4 = Commendable 5 = Superior N/A = Not Applicable

Section III Demonstrated Driving Ability

Employee Name: ______________________ Signature: __________________

Training Officer: ____________________________ Date: ________________

Performance Criteria	Score (Circle One)					
A. Driving						
1. Demonstrates safe, courteous driving at all times	1	2	3	4	5	N/A
2. Smooth acceleration, braking, and turning	1	2	3	4	5	N/A
3. Able to read maps quickly and accurately	1	2	3	4	5	N/A
4. Able to direct partner to locations	1	2	3	4	5	N/A
5. Has knowledge of facilities and locations (New employee may be marginal in category)	1	2	3	4	5	N/A
7. Uses the most direct/expeditious route (New employee may be marginal in category)	1	2	3	4	5	N/A
8. Has headlights on at all times vehicle is in motion.	1	2	3	4	5	N/A
9. Uses turn signals when changing lanes or turning	1	2	3	4	5	N/A
10. Uses seat belts and assures that others use seat belts	1	2	3	4	5	N/A
11. Makes sure all doors are secured before moving	1	2	3	4	5	N/A
12. Turns off interior lights during night driving	1	2	3	4	5	N/A
13. Properly uses emergency warning equipment	1	2	3	4	5	N/A

B. Comments:

Performance Score Definitions

1 = Poor 2 = Marginal 3 = Average 4 = Commendable 5 = Superior N/A = Not Applicable

Section IV Employee Standards

Employee Name: ______________________ Signature: ____________________

Training Officer: ____________________________ Date: __________________

Performance Criteria	Score (Circle One)					
A. Public Relations and Company Rapport						
1. Supportive of patient's family members	1	2	3	4	5	N/A
2. Polite and courteous to general public	1	2	3	4	5	N/A
3. Respectful to medical staff at hospitals	1	2	3	4	5	N/A
4. Respectful to staff at living facilities	1	2	3	4	5	N/A
5. Volunteers when needed to care for patient	1	2	3	4	5	N/A
6. Requests assistance politely when help is needed	1	2	3	4	5	N/A
7. Remains calm and professional in all situations	1	2	3	4	5	N/A
8. Expresses gratitude after each call	1	2	3	4	5	N/A
9. Encourages further business	1	2	3	4	5	N/A
B. Company Policy						
1. Works well with others	1	2	3	4	5	N/A
2. Maintains professional appearance	1	2	3	4	5	N/A
3. Maintains patient confidentiality	1	2	3	4	5	N/A
4. Reports for work promptly	1	2	3	4	5	N/A
5. Understands and follows polices and procedures for scheduling, vacations, overtime, and illnesses	1	2	3	4	5	N/A

C. Comments:

Performance Score Definitions

1 = Poor 2 = Marginal 3 = Average 4 = Commendable 5 = Superior N/A = Not Applicable

Section V — Patient Care

Employee Name: ______________________ Signature: ______________________

Training Officer: ______________________ Date: ______________________

Performance Criteria	Score (Circle One)					
A. Patient Comfort/Compassion						
1. Communicates well with patients	1	2	3	4	5	N/A
2. Displays no prejudice or bias	1	2	3	4	5	N/A
3. Ensures patient comfort in vehicle (temperature)	1	2	3	4	5	N/A
4. Ensures patient comfort on gurney	1	2	3	4	5	N/A
5. Exhibits gentleness when touching/moving patient	1	2	3	4	5	N/A
6. Uses appropriate and professional language	1	2	3	4	5	N/A
7. Strives to make patient happy, relaxed, and comfortable	1	2	3	4	5	N/A
B. Proper Lifting/Moving Techniques						
1. Uses proper lifting techniques, does not lift with back	1	2	3	4	5	N/A
2. Kneels when preparing to lift and assures own safety	1	2	3	4	5	N/A
3. Assures patient safety when moving patient	1	2	3	4	5	N/A
4. Moves patient feet first unless going up hills or stairs	1	2	3	4	5	N/A

C. Comments:

Performance Score Definitions

1 = Poor 2 = Marginal 3 = Average 4 = Commendable 5 = Superior N/A = Not Applicable

Section VI Documentation

Employee Name: ______________________ Signature: __________________

Training Officer: ____________________________ Date: ________________

Performance Criteria	Score (Circle One)					
A. Field/Trip Sheets						
1. Ensures all Trip Sheets are accurate and complete	1	2	3	4	5	N/A
2. Report is written legibly	1	2	3	4	5	N/A
3. Documents all times and mileage correctly	1	2	3	4	5	N/A
B. Incident Reports/Complaints						
1. Understands the "5-W" concept of report writing (who, what, where, when, why)	1	2	3	4	5	N/A

C. Comments:

Performance Score Definitions

1 = Poor 2 = Marginal 3 = Average 4 = Commendable 5 = Superior N/A = Not Applicable

APPENDIX D

Sample Budget Worksheet

Personnel Expenses .... $__________
  Wages and salaries .... $__________
    Justification:
  Overtime .... $__________
    Justification:
  COLA .... $__________
    Justification:
  Payroll taxes .... $__________
    FICA .... __________
    Medicare .... __________
    State unemployment tax .... __________
    State disability insurance .... __________
    Worker's compensation insurance .... __________
  Benefits .... $__________
    Health insurance .... __________
    Justification:
    Dental insurance .... __________
    Justification:
    Life insurance .... __________
    Justification:
    Retirement/pension .... __________
    Justification:

Office Expenses .... $__________
  Rent .... $__________
    Justification:
  Utilities .... $__________
    Telephone—local service .... __________
    Telephone—long distance .... __________
    Telephone—cell phone .... __________
    Electric .... __________
    Water/sewer .... __________
  Postage .... $__________
  Stationery and supplies .... $__________
  Printing/duplicating .... $__________

Justification:
Janitorial services (included in rent) . . . . $__________
Office equipment . . . . $__________
Justification:
Office equipment repair . . . . $__________
Justification:

Travel and Entertainment . . . . **$__________**
Business travel . . . . $__________
Justification:
Business lodging and entertainment . . . . $__________
Justification:
Meals/food . . . . $__________
Justification:

Dues and Subscriptions . . . . **$__________**
Dues . . . . $__________
Justification:
Periodicals . . . . $__________
Justification:
Textbooks and training aids . . . . $__________
Justification:

Education and Training . . . . **$__________**
Travel . . . . $__________
Justification:
Lodging . . . . $__________
Justification:
Meals away from home . . . . $__________
Justification:
Course fees . . . . $__________
Justification:

Equipment . . . . **$__________**
Training equipment . . . . $__________
Mannikins . . . . $__________
Justification:
Projectors . . . . $__________
Soft goods for training (disposable) . . $__________
Repairs and maintenance (estimated) $__________
Vehicle equipment . . . . $__________
Purchased . . . . $__________
Leased @ $300/mo × 12 mo . . . . $__________
Gas, tires, oil @ $0.20/mi ×
15,000 miles . . . . $__________
Insurance, $650/year . . . . $__________
Repairs and maintenance @
$0.16/mi × 15,000 miles . . . . $__________

Total Budget . . . . **$__________**

APPENDIX E

Sample Orientation Schedule for New Employees

Day 1—Orientation to the Office

- Welcome
- Meet the staff
- Organization overview
- Mission statement
- Tour of the office
- Paperwork
  - W-4
  - Other
- Benefits selections
  - Medical
  - Dental
- Office policies and procedures
  - Smoking
  - Workplace violence
  - Emergency preparedness
  - Sexual harassment
  - Employee leaves of absence
  - Employee health and safety

Day 2—Field Operations Policies and Procedures

- Daily vehicle check (with practical exercise)
  - Mechanical
  - Equipment and supplies
  - Reporting mechanical problems
- Radio operations
- Response policies
  - MCI
  - Interfacility transfers
  - Haz-mat responses
  - Patient care policies
  - Local protocols
- Introduction to field training officers
- Roles and responsibilities
- Ride-along assignments

Day 3—Ride-along

Observation of vehicle operations and patient care practices—no active participation

Day 4—Patient Care

Active participation in patient care under supervision of a field training officer

Day 5—Driving

Active participation in vehicle operations under supervision of a field training officer

Performance evaluation review and further recommendations

Index